ENGLISH MEN OF LETTERS

SAMUEL RICHARDSON

D0615476

·The M Co·

SAMUEL RICHARDSON

BY

AUSTIN DOBSON

New York
THE MACMILLAN COMPANY
LONDON: MACMILLAN & CO., Ltd.

1902

Norwood Press
J. S. Cushing & Co. — Berwick & Smith
Norwood Mass. U.S.A.

CONTENTS

A57997

SAMUEL RICHARDSON

CHAPTER I

FROM BIRTH TO AUTHORSHIP

A CLOUD hangs over the cradle of the author of
Clarissa, which he himself has not sought to dissipate.
He was born in 1689, in Derbyshire; but in what place
in that county, he was always, from some obscure
motive, careful to conceal. His father, Samuel Richardson, like the father of Matthew Prior, was a joiner, — a
business, his son informs us, " then more distinct from
that of a carpenter than now it is with us." "He was
a good draughtsman," he adds, " and understood architecture." This, if it is to be taken literally, would mean
that he must have been very much above the ordinary
level of joiners and carpenters.[1] We are told further,
that he was "a very honest man, descended of a family
of middling note, in the county of Surrey, but which
having for several generations a large number of
children, the not large possessions were split and

[1] Mr. Bridgen, Richardson's son-in-law, says " cabinetmakers
were, at that time, called *Joiners*," and he describes the elder
Richardson as "a cabinetmaker, and afterwards a considerable
importer of mahogany, in Aldersgate-street." He also confirms
the statement as to his knowledge of architecture. He " was, in
particular, an excellent Architect."

divided, so that he and his brothers were put to trades; and the sisters were married to tradesmen." " My mother," the record goes on, " was also a good woman, of a family not ungenteel; but whose father and mother died in her infancy, within half-an-hour of each other, in the London pestilence of 1665."

According to his son, the skill and ingenuity of the elder Richardson, coupled with his superior understanding, and " his remarkable integrity of heart and manners," served to recommend him to the special notice of several persons of rank, among whom were the Duke of Monmouth and the first Earl of Shaftesbury. The favour with which he was regarded by these exalted patrons seems however to have become eventually a danger rather than a distinction, since on " the decollation of the first-named unhappy nobleman," Mr. Richardson, senior, " to his great detriment," found himself constrained to give up his London business, and retire to the unnamed retreat in Derbyshire where, with three more out of a total of nine children, his famous son was born.[1] Mrs. Barbauld is perhaps right in concluding that he must have entered more deeply into the political views of the decollated nobleman than he cared to admit, and that it is to this circumstance, rather than to any false pride in connection with the obscurity of his origin, that the persistent reticence of the novelist as to his place of

[1] Mr. Malcolm Kingsley Macmillan, who meditated a *Life of Richardson*, made every effort to discover this place. About 1885, Mr. Macmillan advertised repeatedly in the now defunct *Derby and Derbyshire Gazette*, offering a reward to any parish clerk who would supply conclusive evidence upon the point, but no information was obtained.

birth is to be attributed, — though why, if this be the case, he should have thought it necessary to mention his father's connection with Monmouth at all, is a matter that requires explanation.

However this may be — and the point is not of essential importance to this biography — the Richardson family apparently returned to London at some time after the Revolution, for, according to Nichols's *Literary Anecdotes*, the youthful Samuel is said to have been educated " in the grammar school of Christ's Hospital." But his name is not to be traced in the school registers; and the statement has moreover been held to be inconsistent with the "common-school learning" which he admits to have been his limited equipment. Of this difficulty, Leigh Hunt, who had himself worn the blue gown and yellow stockings, offers what may possibly be regarded as a reasonable solution. "It is a fact not generally known," he says in the *London Journal* (Supp. No. 2, 1834), "that Richardson . . . received what education he had (which was very little, and did not go beyond English) at Christ's Hospital. It may be wondered how he could come no better taught from a school which had sent forth so many good scholars; but in his time, and indeed till very lately, that foundation was divided into several schools, none of which partook of the lessons of the others; and Richardson, agreeably to his father's intention of bringing him up to trade, was most probably confined to the writing-school, where all that was taught was writing and arithmetic." Leigh Hunt has the reputation of being an extremely conscientious investigator. He is not likely to have spoken without warranty; and, in any case, his statements serve to show that it was possible to be educated at Christ's Hospital with very modest results.[1]

Of Richardson's school days, however, whether at Christ's Hospital or elsewhere, we know nothing save what he himself has told us. But he must clearly have been born with that bias which Emerson regarded as a man's crowning boon from fortune. He was to succeed as a story-teller, and he is a story-teller " e'en from his boyish days." " I recollect," he says, " that I was early noted for having invention. I was not fond of play, as other boys; my school-fellows used to call me *Serious* and *Gravity*; and five of them particularly delighted to single me out, either for a walk, or at their father's houses, or at mine, to tell them stories, as they phrased it. Some I told them, from my reading, as true; others from my head, as mere invention; of which they would be most fond, and often were affected by them. One of them particularly, I remember, was for putting me to write a history, as he called it, on the model of Tommy Pots; I now forget what it was, only that it was of a servant-man preferred by a fine young lady (for his goodness) to a lord, who was a libertine. All my stories carried with them, I am bold to say, an useful moral."

Mrs. Barbauld points out that a subsequent translator of *Pamela* and *Clarissa*, M. Prévost, the author of *Manon Lescaut*, was wont in like manner to amuse the Carthusians of his convent with stories of his contriving; though it may be doubted whether these were of the

---

[1] The matter is still very doubtful; for against Leigh Hunt must be placed the statement of Mr. Bridgen that " it is certain that he [Richardson] was never sent to a more respectable seminary " than " a private grammar school " in Derbyshire.

type of Tommy Pots. But it was part of the bias
with which Richardson was born, that he also, in his
earliest youth, exhibited the less common proclivity
towards letter-writing. Even in his childhood he was
copious in his "epistolary correspondence," and his
facility in this way must sometimes have been a source
of embarrassment, and even annoyance, to those about
him. Before he was eleven, he wrote an expostulatory
letter to a back-biting widow of near fifty, who,
pretending to religion, was nevertheless continually
fomenting quarrels and disturbances. He drew up a
formidable array of appropriate texts, and, "assuming
the style and address of a person in years," warned her
of the error of her ways. The letter, of course, was
anonymous. But his handwriting was detected, and
the recipient of the lecture complained bitterly, and
not unnaturally, to the lad's mother. "My mother
chid me for the freedom taken by such a boy with
a woman of her years; but knowing that her son was
not of a pert or forward nature, but, on the contrary, shy and bashful, she commended my principles,
though she censured the liberty taken." It will be
noted that the grown man who penned this reminis-
cence seems to have had no shadow of misgiving as to
the very priggish action of the boy.

Another of Richardson's characteristics closely
allied to those already mentioned, may best be
referred to in his own language. "I was an early
favourite with all the young women of taste and
reading in the neighbourhood. Half a dozen of them,
when met to work with their needles, used, when
they got a book they liked, and thought I should, to
borrow me to read to them; their mothers sometimes

with them; and both mothers and daughters used to be pleased with the observations they put me on making."

"I was not more than thirteen, when some of these young women, unknown to each other, having a high opinion of my taciturnity, revealed to me their love-secrets, in order to induce me to give them copies to write after, or correct, for answers to their lover's letters: nor did any one of them ever know that I was the secretary to the others. I have been directed to chide, and even repulse, when an offence was either taken or given, at the very time that the heart of the chider or repulser was open before me, overflowing with esteem and affection; and the fair repulser, dreading to be taken at her word, directing *this* word, or *that* expression, to be softened or changed. One highly gratified with her lover's fervour, and vows of everlasting love, has said, when I have asked her direction; I cannot tell you what to write; but (her heart on her lips), you cannot write too kindly; all her fear was only, that she should incur slight for her kindness."

Literary history, like other history, has a trick of repeating itself, and it has been whispered that a distinguished novelist of our own day, Mr. Thomas Hardy, held a somewhat similar office in his Wessex home, although, to be sure, he was the penman rather than the composer of the letters. The value to Richardson of this elementary school of passion must have been considerable, but it would perhaps be rash to conclude that he found more than Pamela in this early environment. Clarissa and Clementina would be later growths. So much, indeed, he himself admits to the Dutch minister, Mr. J. Stinstra, who, in 1753, had asked him where he had obtained his accurate knowledge of humanity. "You think, Sir, you can account from my early secretaryship to young women in my father's neighbourhood, for the characters I have drawn of the heroines of my three works. But this opportunity did little more for me, at so tender an age, than point, as I may say, or lead my enquiries, as I grew up, into the knowledge of the female heart." That is to say, when he wrote *Pamela*, he had only "prospected" the country : when he wrote *Clarissa*, he had become a scientific explorer. And then he goes on to make certain observations with respect to that other untravelled region, the male heart, to which it may be useful to return hereafter.

The first intention of the elder Richardson had been to make his son a clergyman, a calling for which the boy had obvious qualifications. But owing to losses he sustained, he was unable to give him the requisite education, and he accordingly left him, at fifteen or sixteen, to choose a business for himself. Young Richardson selected that of a printer, chiefly, he alleges, because he thought it would allow him to gratify a thirst for reading, which, in after years, he disclaimed. In 1706, being then seventeen, he was apprenticed to Mr. John Wilde of Stationers' Hall and Aldersgate Street. No picturesque reminiscences of this eventful portion of his life are forthcoming. Whether he was subjected to any of those mysterious rites which, as related in the veracious Memoirs of his contemporary, and subsequent assistant, Thomas Gent, accompanied, in printing-house "Chapels," the admission of a neophyte to the privileges of "Cuzship"; — whether he "dangled after his mistress, with the great gilt Bible under his arm, to St. Bride's, on a Sunday, brought home the text, repeated the divisions of the discourse, dined at twelve, and regaled, upon a gaudy day, with buns and beer at Islington, or Mile-End"—like his crop-eared fellow in Foote's *Minor*—no biographer has told us. It may, nevertheless, be safely asserted that he did *not*, like Hogarth's Thomas Idle, tear his *'Prentice's Guide*, and peruse instead the profane broadside ballads of what Gent calls the "wide-mouthed, stentorian hawkers." On the contrary, there is good ground, as we shall see presently, for concluding that, like Francis Goodchild, he duly shared his hymn-book at church with his master's daughter, and otherwise foreshadowed and anticipated the career of that excellent and exemplary young man.

But although, in Mr. Wilde's shop, the "stream ran by his lips"—to use Mrs. Barbauld's poetical figure—he did not, during his probation, find it very easy to gratify his thirst for reading. "I served," he says of his apprenticeship, "a diligent seven years to it; to a master who grudged every hour to me that tended not to his profit, even of those times of leisure and diversion, which the refractoriness of my fellow-servants *obliged* him to allow them, and were usually allowed by other masters to their apprentices. I stole from the hours of rest and relaxation, my reading times for improvement of my mind; and, being engaged in correspondence with a gentleman, greatly my superior in degree, and of ample fortune, who, had he lived, intended high things for me; these were all the opportunities I had in my apprenticeship to carry it on. But this little incident I may mention;

I took care that even my candle was of my own pur-
chasing, that I might not, in the most trifling instance,
make my master a sufferer (and who used to call me
the pillar of his house) and not to disable myself by
watching or sitting-up, to perform my duty to him
in the day time." The unknown gentleman's letters,
it appears subsequently, related mainly to his own
travels and transactions; he was "a master of the
epistolary style," and his curious fancy for corresponding with a city printer's apprentice who wanted
practice in pen-craft, might have supplied the Philos-
opher Square with a fresh illustration of the " eternal
fitness of things." Eventually the gentleman died,
depriving his young friend of a valuable patron ; and
by request, the letters, on both sides, were burned.
But, as far as Richardson was concerned, they served
their turn by giving readiness and fluency to his
natural habit of the pen. They may even have done
more. " Early familiar Letter-writing," he said later
in *Clarissa*, " is one of the greatest openers and
improvers of the mind that man or woman can be
employed in."

If his apprenticeship began in 1706 and lasted seven
years, it must have come to an end in 1713. For five
or six years more he continued to work as a compositor
and corrector of the press, and part of the time as an
overseer. Then, in 1719, he took up his freedom, and
began business as a master printer in an unidentified
court in Fleet Street, filling his spare time by the preparation for the booksellers of prefaces, indexes, and
what he terms vaguely "honest dedications." It is
probably to this occupation that we owe the elaborate
Collection of the Moral and Instructive Sentiments, etc.,

*contained in the Histories of Pamela, Clarissa, and Sir
Charles Grandison,* which he prepared in later life to
accompany those novels.   In 1721, two years after he
had set up for himself, he confirmed his resemblance to
Hogarth's " Industrious Apprentice " by marrying the
daughter of his old master, John Wilde.   This, with
the exception that she gave the wrong Christian name
to the lady, was Mrs. Barbauld's original statement,
although some recent authorities, relying on Nichols's
Literary Anecdotes, have preferred to believe that his
father-in-law was one Allington Wilde of Clerkenwell.
But Richardson's latest biographer, Miss Clara Thomson, has shown conclusively that, — as is moreover
apparent from Richardson's will,—Allington Wilde was
his brother-in-law, and that his wife, Martha Wilde, to
whom, by the registers of Charterhouse Chapel, he was
married on the 23rd November 1721, was the daughter
of John Wilde of Aldersgate Street and Martha A.
Allington, after whom Mrs. Richardson's brother was
no doubt named.

" It's not Mrs. Brown that lies there," writes
Thackeray's Brown the Elder, explaining dolefully
to Brown the Younger that a certain sarcophagus at
Funchal does *not* enclose his late aunt's remains.   Probably Martha Wilde, too, had predecessors, although
we need perhaps scarcely go as far as to conclude
with Miss Thomson that Richardson's marriage was
" prompted mainly by prudential considerations."   But
from a sentimentalist, sentiment must be expected,
and in a later letter to a correspondent, he more than
hints at previous love-affairs, which, apart from the
fact that, owing to his bashfulness, they seem always
to have originated with the weaker sex, had also the

drawback of being generally impracticable. " A pretty ideot," he writes, " was once proposed, with very high terms, his [Richardson's] circumstances considered; her worthy uncle thought this man [R. again] would behave compassionately to her. — A violent Roman Catholic lady was another, of a fine fortune, a zealous professor ; whose terms were (all her fortune in her own power — a very apron-string tenure !) two years' probation, and her confessor's report in favour of his being a true proselyte at the end of them.— Another, a gay, high-spirited, volatile lady, whose next friend offered to be *his* friend, in fear of her becoming the prey (at the public places she constantly frequented) of some vile fortune-hunter.   Another there was whom his soul loved ; but with a reverence — Hush ! — Pen, lie thee down ! " — And then comes what the writer elsewhere describes as " an interrupting sigh," and " a short abruption."   Mrs. Barbauld, who thinks that the " violent Roman Catholic lady " may have given the first hint of Clementina in *Sir Charles Grandison*, adds that the tender circumstances last hinted at were supposed by the novelist's friends to be obscurely shadowed out in *The History of Mrs. Beaumont*, which she prints at the end of her fifth volume, and which Richardson could never relate without a certain suspicious animation.   But his personal love-affairs, as far as they have been revealed to us, possess but slender biographical importance, and certainly lack the element of romance which he was able to infuse into his stories.

Beyond the births successively of six children, all of whom but one, a boy, died in infancy, there is little to chronicle in Richardson's life for the next few years.

Almost the only notable incident between his first marriage and the publication of *Pamela*, was his brief connection with *The True Briton*, a bi-weekly political paper established by Philip, Duke of Wharton, in June 1723 (just before the exile of Atterbury), in opposition to the Government, and in the interests of the Jacobites. This, which was published by T. Payne, near Stationers' Hall, was at first printed by Richardson, whose name, fortunately for himself, did not appear, since an information was speedily lodged against the publisher in regard to Nos. 3, 4, 5, and 6 as being more than " common libels." It is suggested by Nichols in his *Literary Anecdotes* that No. 6, which refers, among other things, to the Bishop of Rochester, may have been written by Richardson himself. But Wharton's biographer, Mr. J. R. Robinson, plainly attributes it to Wharton; and it is extremely improbable that Richardson's cautious, and even timorous nature would have permitted him to put pen to any performance of the kind. It is still more improbable that the obscure printer of *The True Briton*, with which, moreover, he prudently severed his connection at the above-mentioned sixth number, could ever have been on really intimate terms with the brilliant and witty profligate, whose portrait after Jervas, coupled with " His Grace's PROTEST against the Bill for Inflicting certain Pains and Penalties on *Francis* late Lord Bishop of *Rochester*," was at the time in all the print-shops ; and who, two years later, left England for ever. Yet not only has it been suggested that Richardson had special opportunities for studying refined libertinism in the person of Wharton, but that he obtained a sufficient acquaintance with his character to make him, a quarter of a century later, the prototype of Robert Lovelace. This surely can be no more than the exaggeration of the desire which must find an original for everything. That certain lines of Pope's character of Wharton in the Epistle to Lord Cobham, and notably —

" Women and Fools must like him or he dies "—

might be applied to Clarissa's betrayer, is no doubt true ; but they might also be applied with equal truth to Rowe's Lothario (a much more likely model for Lovelace !) or to the Don Juan of Molière. When Richardson drew his cold-blooded hero, Wharton had been dead for seventeen years ; and he himself had been studying human nature in too many places to need to fall back upon his recollections of a meteoric rake of quality, whom he may never even have encountered in the flesh. For what knowledge does the anonymous setter-up of treasonable political matter obtain of the writer who prepares the "copy"! One has only to turn to the life of another, though perhaps humbler, contemporary printer, Thomas Gent of York, to note with what meticulous precautions, about this very time, this same Bishop of Rochester to whom reference has been made, surrounded the issue of a private pamphlet. Gent never knew who his employer was, until he afterwards recognised him on his way to the Tower as a prisoner.

In 1724 Richardson moved from Fleet Street into Salisbury Square, or, as it was then called, Salisbury Court, where he occupied a house " in the centre " of the Court now no longer in existence. Oddly enough the next circumstance to be recorded in his career comes from the records of the above-mentioned Thomas Gent. "After this," says Gent, speaking of a date following the return of George I. from Hanover in 1724, "Mr. Woodfall [*i.e.* the first of that name] was so kind [as] to recommend me to the ingenious Mr. Richardson, in Salisbury Court; with whom I staid to finish his part of the Dictionary which he had from the booksellers, composed of English, Latin, Greek, and Hebrew." But Richardson found a better friend than either Wharton or Henry Woodfall in Arthur Onslow, the Speaker of the House of Commons, through whom he was employed to print the Journals of the House, a first instalment of twenty-six volumes of which he duly completed. Mr. Onslow seems to have had a benevolent regard for his protégé, and frequently entertained him at that pleasant Ember or Imber Court by the Mole at Thames Ditton, which he had acquired in 1720 on his marriage to Miss Ann Bridges. But, as Mrs. Barbauld pertinently observes, "polite regards are sometimes more easily obtained than money from the court end of the town. Mr. R. did not find this branch of his business the one which yielded him the quickest returns. He thus writes to his friend Aaron Hill : ' As to my silence, I have been at one time exceedingly busy in getting ready some volumes of Journals, to entitle myself to a payment which yet I never had, no, not to the value of a shilling, though the debt is upwards of three thousand pounds, and though I have pressed for it, and been excessively pressed for the want of it.'" His position as Printer of the Journals of the House of Commons must, nevertheless, have brought him work in other ways.

On the 25th January 1731, Martha Richardson died, her death being hastened by the death of one of her children, perhaps the boy William, who lived to be four years old.　In the following year Richardson married Elizabeth Leake, sister of James Leake, a bookseller at Bath, and no doubt the " J. Leake," whose name appears, with those of Rivington and John Osborn, on the title-page of the book known generally as the *Familiar Letters*.　By his second wife he had several daughters, four of whom, Mary, Martha, Anne, and Sarah, as will be seen hereafter, survived their father.　A " promising boy," Samuel, was born in 1739 and died in 1740.　Richardson seems to have been an affectionate father, and his many bereavements did not tend to improve his health, or diminish his nervous sensibility.　From 1736 to 1737 he was the printer of the *Daily Journal*, and in 1738 of the *Daily Gazetteer*. In the former of these years he was also appointed printer to a so-called " Society for the Encouragement of Learning," which, among other things, was intended to make authors independent of publishers.　But even a ducal President, titled Trustees, and a paid Secretary were ineffectual to float the enterprise, and it eventually collapsed for want of a Besant to keep it going.

" He, they say, who is not handsome by Twenty, strong by Thirty, wise by Forty, rich by Fifty, will never be either *handsome, strong, wise,* or *rich*."　Thus writes Richardson at p. 92 of the *Familiar Letters*.　At this date, the question of strength and good looks had, in his case, long been settled.　He was a weakly and nervous valetudinarian, already wedded to a special diet.　As to wisdom, he had learned a good deal of prudence and common sense in his business; and in

spite of deferred Government payments, must have
been, at fifty, his age in 1739, well-to-do and comfortable as to his means.   Already he had begun, after
the fashion of the prosperous citizens of his day, to
indulge himself with a country residence, to which,
like the tradesman in No. xxxiii. of the *Connois-
seur,* he retired from Saturday to Monday.   One of the
unpublished letters addressed to him in July 1736,
speaks of a retreat called Corney House, which may
have been a house of that name by the waterside at
Chiswick, and may also have been in some other
suburb.   But in 1739 he took a lease of part of
another house, then in the open country, close to
Hammersmith turnpike ; and now known as No. 111
(formerly No. 49), The Grange, North End Road,
Fulham.   The Grange had originally been built about
1714 by a certain John, or Justice Smith, on the site
of two cottages dating from the time of Charles II.
It consisted of two houses, in the northernmost of
which Justice Smith lived until his death in 1725, at
which time the other, or south house, was occupied
jointly by the Countess of Ranelagh (widow of the
first Earl of Ranelagh) and a Mr. Samuel Vanderplank,
often mentioned in Richardson's letters.   Richardson,
as already stated, took up his residence in the North
House in 1739.   It was well arranged and roomy (he
says in one of his letters that he could make ten beds,
and give guests a separate parlour) ; and, as to its
environment, naturally far less hedged in by buildings
than it is at present.   The annual rent he paid to
Mr. Vanderplank was twenty-five pounds.   At the
back of the house was a pleasant garden, which contained an historical grotto or summer-house, where, as

we shall see, he was wont to work and read his productions to his admirers. Of this grotto no trace is now left, and it is supposed to have disappeared in 1801. In vol. iv. of Mrs. Barbauld's edition of the correspondence, there is an engraving of the twin houses by T. Richards, which shows them as they looked about 1800, but alterations in the windows, the addition of a balcony, and the facing of the northern portion with stucco have made it difficult to reconcile its past with its present appearance. The name, The Grange, dates from 1836. What its first name was, and what especially was its name when, from 1739 to 1754, its tenant was Richardson, have not been ascertained. One of the novelist's correspondents, a Mr. Reich, of Leipzig — who must have visited him towards the close of his tenancy, since he refers to *Sir Charles Grandison* as already existent — speaks of it as " Selby House "; but as this is the house in which the Miss Byron of the novel spent her girlhood, it is doubtful whether it was more than a playful appellation. Such as it was, however, the northern half of The Grange was Richardson's country home for fifteen years, or until he moved to Parson's Green. He kept one maid-servant there all the year round; he sent others to stay there when they were out of health; and as he grew older, he lived there himself for much longer periods than the mere week-ends which had at first been the limits of his escape from the bustle of Salisbury Court.[1]

[1] The Grange, after other tenants, was, from 1867 to 1898, the residence of Sir E. Burne-Jones, Bart., the distinguished painter. It is now in the occupation of Mr. Fairfax Murray. Many of the above particulars as to the history of the house are derived from vol. ii. of the exhaustive *Fulham Old and New* of Mr. Charles James Feret, 1900.

When, in 1739, Richardson took his Hammersmith house, he had, notwithstanding his advanced age, done little in literature save the dedications and indexes to which reference has been made. It is probable, however, that, about this time, he was already occupied in editing, for the above-mentioned Society for the Encouragement of Literature, a part of the correspondence of Sir Thomas Roe relating to his embassy to the Ottoman Porte. But it is to 1739 that belongs the book which undoubtedly prompted *Pamela*, and which — partly from its having fallen into neglect, and partly also from the perhaps intentionally vague way in which he himself speaks of a production his subsequent successes made him willing to forget — has sometimes been confused with *Pamela* itself. In 1739, two of his particular friends, Mr. Charles Rivington of St. Paul's Churchyard, and Mr. John Osborn of Paternoster Row, invited him to prepare for them " a little volume of Letters, in a common style, on such subjects as might be of use to those country readers, who were unable to indite for themselves. Will it be any harm, said I, in a piece you want to be written so low, if we should instruct them how they should think and act in common cases, as well as indite ? They were the more urgent with me to begin the little volume for this hint. I set about it. . . . "

At this point, both for clearness' sake and the avoidance of misconception, it will be well to adopt Richardson's plan of " a short abruption," and go on with the story of the volume initiated by Messrs. Osborn and Rivington. With these model letters, as already stated, originated the idea of Richardson's first novel of *Pamela*. It is true that they were not

published until a few weeks after *Pamela* had appeared;
but as they undoubtedly preceded that book in conception, and probably in execution, they may legiti-
mately be treated first. They appeared in January
1741 (*Pamela* having been issued in the preceding
November), and their full title is as follows: *Letters
written to and for particular Friends, on the most important Occasions. Directing not only the requisite Style
and Forms to be observed in writing* Familiar Letters;
*but how to think and act justly and prudently, in the
common Concerns of Human Life.* The title moreover
states that the volume contains "One Hundred and
Seventy-three Letters, None of which were ever before
Published"; and it was "printed for C. Rivington,
in St. Paul's Churchyard; J. Osborn, in Pater-noster
Row; and J. Leake, at Bath "—this last, no doubt,
being Richardson's brother-in-law. The price was two
shillings and sixpence, and the *Gentleman's Magazine,*
in which it is advertised, reproduced, at page 34 of
its eleventh volume, one of the letters—"Advice to
a Friend against going to Law " (No. 144). Mr. Urban
gives no hint as to the author, whose " Preface " lays
stress upon his having, among other things, devoted
exceptional attention to the details of discreet court-
ship and the disadvantages of ill-considered matrimony.
" *Orphans,* and *Ladies* of *independent Fortunes,* he [the
compiler] has particularly endeavour'd to guard against
the insidious Arts of their *flattering* and *selfish* Depen-
dents, and the *clandestine* Addresses of *Fortune-hunters,*
those Beasts of Prey, as they may well be called, who
spread their *Snares* for the *innocent* and *thoughtless*
Heart." The management of this final metaphor is
not perhaps of the happiest. As we have seen, how-

ever, in the case of the "high-spirited volatile lady"
who wished to marry the author, the eighteenth-
century fortune-hunter was distinctly a danger to be
reckoned with.

But while the affairs of the heart naturally occupy
a considerable portion of the *Familiar Letters*, — we
should imagine indeed that there can be few complications arising from the undisciplined employment of
that organ which are left untreated, — many of these
fictitious utterances show clearly that, from his Fleet
Street shop, Richardson had looked not unintelligently
upon life in general.   Indeed, in regard to the question
of the law's delays, it might almost be conjectured
that he was still smarting under an unfavourable
personal experience.   Here is the close of his epistle
to the would-be litigant : — " Then you may be plung'd
into the bottomless Gulf of Chancery, where you
begin with Bills and Answers, containing Hundreds
of Sheets at exorbitant Prices, 15 Lines in a Sheet,
and 6 Words in a Line, (and a Stamp to every Sheet)
barefacedly so contrived to pick your Pocket : Then
follow all the Train of Examinations, Interrogatories,
Exceptions, Bills amended, References for Scandal and
Impertinence, new Allegations, new Interrogatories,
new Exceptions, on Pretence of insufficient Answers,
Replies, Rejoinders, Sur-rejoinders, Butters, Rebutters,
and Sur-rebutters ; till, at last, when you have danc'd
thro' this blessed Round of *Preparation*, the *Tryal*
before the Master of the Rolls comes next; Appeals
follow from his Honour to the Chancellor ; then from
the Chancellor to the House of Lords ; and sometimes
the Parties are sent from thence for a new Tryal in
the Courts below — Good Heavens !   What wise Man,

permit me to repeat, would enter himself into this
confounding *Circle of the Law?*"

Here, from another letter, is a "prospect" of contemporary politics, which reminds one of some of the
later deliverances of Fielding in the *Covent Garden
Journal:*—" For while some are made as *black* as *Devils*
on one Side, they are made as *white* as *Angels* on the
other. They never did *one good thing*, says the *Enemy.*
They never did *one bad* one, says the *Friend.* . . .
Mean time one Side goes on, *accusing* without *Mercy;*
the other, *acquitting* without *Shame.* 'Tis the Business
of *one Set* of Papers to *bespatter* and *throw Dirt;* and
of the *other* to follow after them, with a *Scrubbing-
brush* and a *Dish-clout:* And after all — the one *bedaubs*
so *plentifully*, and the other *wipes* off so *slovenly*, that,
let me be hang'd, *Bob*, if I'd appear on *'Change* with
the Coat on my Back that a certain great Man stalks
about in, without Concern, when these *Dawbers* and
Scowerers have done their *worst* and their *best* upon
it. But 'tis a great Matter to be *used* to such a Coat.
And a great Happiness, I'll warrant, your Namesake
[Sir Robert Walpole] thinks it, that with all this
Rubbing and *Scrubbing*, it does not appear *threadbare*
yet, after twenty Years' Wear, and a hundred People
trying to pick Holes in it."

If personal experiences have dictated some of these
communications, personal predilections peep out in
others. The writer is severe in matters of costume.
"I have been particularly offended, let me tell you,
my Dear [he writes to a young lady], at your *new
Riding Habit*, which is made so extravagantly in the
Mode, that one cannot easily distinguish your Sex
by it. For you neither look like a *modest Girl* in it,

nor an *agreeable Boy*. Some conformity to the Fashion
is allowable. But a cock'd Hat, a lac'd Jacket, a
Fop's Peruke, what strange Metamorphoses do they
make!" Elsewhere, he courageously lifts up his voice
against the undue "Love of Singing and Musick."
"It may tend," he tells an imaginary correspondent,
"for so it naturally does, to *enervate the Mind*, and
make you haunt musical Societies, Operas and Con-
certs; and what Glory is it to a Gentleman if he were
even a fine Performer, that he can strike a String,
touch a Key, or sing a Song with the Grace and
Command of a *hired Musician*?" Upon the topic of
the Stage he is even less sympathetic. He does not,
indeed, like Goldsmith to his brother-in-law, Hodson,
brand acting as "an abominable resource which neither
becomes a man of honour, nor a man of sense," but
in the character of a Father whose Son, "reduced by
his own Extravagance," wishes to turn player, he
writes as follows: "You must consider, that tho' in
the gay Trappings of that Employment a Man may
represent a Gentleman, yet none can be farther from
that Character if a perpetual Dependence be the worst
Kind of Servility. In the first Place, the Company
you will be in a manner obliged to keep, will be such as
will tend little to the Improvement of your Mind, or
Amendment of your Morals : To the Master of the Company you list in, you must be obsequious to a Degree of
Slavery. Not one of an Audience that is able to *hiss*,[1]
but you must *fear*, and each single Person you come to

---

[1] *Cf*. Johnson's Prologue to Goldsmith's *Good Natur'd
Man :* —

> " This night, our wit, the pert apprentice cries,
> Lies at my feet, I hiss him, and he dies."

know personally, you must oblige on every Occasion that Offers, to engage their Interest at your Benefit." He will, moreover, have " the mortifying Knowledge of being deem'd a Vagrant by the Laws of his Country."

Many of the other letters have characteristic touches. A Sea Officer, writing to his wife from abroad, sends her a " small Parcel of *Cyprus* wine " ; while a Sailor, not to be behind-hand, forwards to his Peggy from Barbadoes, " as a Token of my Love," six bottles of Citron-water,[1] which " is what, they say, Ladies drink, when they can get it." To which Peggy returns, in the true " Rule Britannia " vein, — " Let who will speak against *Sailors;* they are the Glory and the Safeguard of the Land. And what would have become of *Old England* long ago but for *them?* I am sure the lazy good-for-nothing *Land-lubbers* would never have protected us from our cruel Foes." Another passage shows a Fielding-like appreciation of the wrongs of the " inferior clergy." " Parson *Matthews* goes on preaching and living excellently, and has still as many Admirers as Hearers, but no preferment: While old clumsy Parson *Dromedary* is made a Dean, and has Hopes, by his Sister's means, who is a Favourite of a certain great Man, to be a Bishop." Towards the end of the book are eleven letters from " a young Lady in Town to her Aunt in the Country," describing the sights of London and Westminster. These, in some respects, are the most interesting in the collection. Vauxhall, of course, is visited, and the writer sits in one of the

---

[1] " Plenty of Barbadoes-water for the ladies " — was, it will be remembered, considerately provided by Lieut. Hatchway for Commodore Trunnion's wedding supper (*Peregrine Pickle;* ch. ix.).

famous supper-boxes in the Grove, which is decorated
by a scene from Hippisley's *Hob in the Well*. At
Westminster Abbey, she censures Mat Prior's monu-
ment as " a sad Instance of Pride beyond the Grave ! "
and condemns, very properly, Gay's flippant epitaph
on himself. As regards Sir Cloudesley Shovel, she
follows Addison, which shows that Richardson must
have read his *Spectator* more diligently than he would
have Cave to believe : " I thought (says the writer of the
letter) he [the Admiral] was a rough *honest Tar;* yet
his Effigies makes him a *great Beau,* with a fine flowing
full-bottomed Periwig, such a one, but much finer, and
more in Buckle, than that we have seen our Lawyer
Mr. *Kettleby* [1] wear at our Assizes." At Bedlam, to
which, like the ladies in the *Rake's Progress*, she also
goes, she has the unpleasant experience of being mistaken by one of the Patients for the particular " Betty
Careless " who is the cause of his anguish. " No sooner
did I put my Face to the Grate, but he leap'd from his
Bed, and called me, with frightful Fervency, to come
into his Room. . . . My Cousin assured me such
Fancies were frequent upon these Occasions." [2] At
the Play, she witnesses *Hamlet,* and is justly severe
upon " the low Scenes of *Harlequinery*," by which it was
followed. Finally, there is a letter, not of this series,

---

[1] It is strange that in these model epistles, Richardson should
mention a real personage. Kettleby, whose full-bottomed wig
is historical, was a subscriber to Fielding's *Miscellanies* of 1743 ;
is mentioned in the *Causidicade ;* and was, by many, identified as
the Parson of Hogarth's *Midnight Modern Conversation.*

[2] Until late in the Eighteenth Century Bedlam was a show and
place of meeting. Visitors were admitted for a penny each ; and
John Taylor says that his father courted his mother there (*Records
of my Life*, 1832, i. 3).

which graphically describes "Execution Day," with all the horrors of that "Diversion of the Populace" against which Fielding and other contemporaries so persistently appealed. There is a passage in it which might have come direct from the autobiography of the "Prisoner's Chaplain," Silas Told. "One of the Bodies was carried to the Lodging of his Wife, who not being in the way to receive it, they [the Mob] immediately hawked it about to every Surgeon they could think of ; and when none would buy it, they rubb'd Tar all over it, and left it in a Field hardly cover'd with Earth."

Richardson was ashamed of the *Familiar Letters*. He seems never to have added to them, for the number given in the seventh edition, published after his death, with his name, is the same as that in the first, viz. : — one hundred and seventy-three. "This volume of letters" — he wrote to a friend — "is not worthy of your perusal." They [the letters] were "intended for the lower classes of people," — he says again in another place; and Mrs. Barbauld observes that the book is "seldom found any where but in the servant's drawer." Why it should take refuge there in particular, is not clear, since it is not exclusively calculated for the meridian of the kitchen. Nor is it clear why Jeffrey in his review of Mrs. Barbauld's book in the *Edinburgh* for October 1804, should especially recommend it as likely to be "of singular use to Mr. Wordsworth and his friends in their great scheme of turning all our poetry into the language of the common people." In both cases it would seem as if the writers knew little experimentally of the work referred to.

CHAPTER II

In the preceding chapter, Richardson's account of the origin of his first novel was purposely suspended in order to pursue the story of the collection of *Familiar Letters* which he had undertaken to prepare for Messrs. Rivington and Osborn. That account is now resumed. "In the progress of it [the collection]," — he goes on to say, — "writing two or three letters to instruct handsome girls, who were obliged to go out to service, as we phrase it, how to avoid the snares that might be laid against their virtue," — a story which he had heard many years before recurred to his thoughts. "And hence sprung *Pamela*." "Little did I think, at first," he adds elsewhere, "of making one, much less two volumes of it." . . . "I thought the story, if written in an easy and natural manner, suitably to the simplicity of it, might possibly introduce a new species of writing, that might possibly turn young people into a course of reading different from the pomp and parade of romance-writing, and dismissing the improbable and marvellous, with which novels generally abound, might tend to promote the cause of religion and virtue." His wife, with a young lady friend who lived with them, grew interested in the book during its progress, and were in the habit of

26

coming every evening to his little writing-closet with, " Have you any more of Pamela, Mr. R. ? We are come to hear a little more of Pamela," etc. With this encouragement from his " worthy-hearted " better-half and her companion, *Pamela* got on so fast that, begun on 10th November 1739, it was finished 10th January 1740. Mrs. Barbauld makes this three months. It was only two; and the fact that, in the intervals of a business to which he was devoted, its author contrived to produce two volumes of 296 and 396 pages each so rapidly, is no mean testimony to the fertility of his imagination and the promptitude of his pen.[1]

Which of the epistles to young women first set him on his task, is not now discernible. The *Familiar Letters* of 1741 contain at least three which bear indirectly upon this theme. One is No. cxxviii., headed : " A Father to a Daughter in Service, on hearing of her Master's attempting her Virtue," and it is followed by the daughter's reply ; a third, No. lxii., relates the experiences of a young girl, who, coming to town without friends, narrowly escapes the fate of the heroine of Hogarth's famous Progress, and her " shocking Story " is authenticated by a note stating that it is " Fact in every Circumstance," taken from the mouth of the young girl herself.[2] But the incident

[1] In an unpublished letter to Aaron Hill at South Kensington, he adds some particulars to this account. " For twenty Years I had proposed to different Persons (who thought the Subject too humble for them) that of Pamela ; and it was owing to an Accident (The writing the little Piece of Familiar Letters) that I entered upon it myself. And its strange Success at Publication is still my Surprize." (26 Jan. 1746-7).

[2] That these dangers of Eighteenth-Century London were not wholly the growth of Richardson's imagination, is clear from an anecdote given in Dr. John Brown's *Horæ Subsecivæ*, 1862, p. 25.

which proximately inspired Richardson, and which
(as Scott suggests) was probably derived from the
corresponding gentleman of his 'prentice days, is
related by him in one of his letters to Aaron Hill.
As it serves to explain the subject of the novel, it may
be given here in Richardson's own words: —

"I will now write to your question — Whether there
was any original groundwork of fact, for the general
foundation of Pamela's story.

"About twenty-five years ago, a gentleman, with
whom I was intimately acquainted (but who, alas! is
now no more!) met with such a story as that of
Pamela, in one of the summer tours which he used
to take for his pleasure, attended with one servant
only. At every inn he put up at, it was his way
to inquire after curiosities in its neighbourhood, either
ancient or modern; and particularly he asked who
was the owner of a fine house, as it seemed to him,
beautifully situated, which he had passed by (describing it) within a mile or two of the inn.

"It was a fine house, the landlord said. The owner
was Mr. B. a gentleman of a large estate in more
counties than one. That his and his lady's history
engaged the attention of everybody who came that
way, and put a stop to all other inquiries, though the
house and gardens were well worth seeing. The lady,
he said, was one of the greatest beauties in England;
but the qualities of her mind had no equal: beneficent,
prudent, and equally beloved by high and low. That
she had been taken at twelve years of age, for the
sweetness of her manners and modesty, and for an
understanding above her years, by Mr. B ——'s mother,
a truly worthy lady, to wait on her person. Her

parents, ruined by suretiships, were remarkably honest and pious, and had instilled into their daughter's mind the best principles. When their misfortunes happened first, they attempted a little school, in their village, where they were much beloved; he teaching writing and the first rules of arithmetic to boys, his wife plain needlework to girls, and to knit and spin; but that it answered not; and when the lady took their child, the industrious man earned his bread by day labour, and the lowest kinds of husbandry.

"That the girl, improving daily in beauty, modesty, and genteel and good behaviour, by the time she was fifteen, engaged the attention of her lady's son, a young gentleman of free principles, who, on her lady's death, attempted, by all manner of temptations and devices, to seduce her. That she had recourse to as many innocents stratagems to escape the snares laid for her virtue; once, however, in despair, having been near drowning; that, at last, her noble resistance, watchfulness, and excellent qualities, subdued him, and he thought fit to make her his wife. That she behaved herself with so much dignity, sweetness, and humility, that she made herself beloved of everybody, and even by his relations, who at first despised her; and now had the blessings both of rich and poor, and the love of her husband.

"The gentleman who told me this, added, that he had the curiosity to stay in the neighbourhood from Friday to Sunday, that he might see this happy couple at church, from which they never absented themselves: that, in short, he did see them; that her deportment was all sweetness, ease, and dignity mingled: that he never saw a lovelier woman: that her husband was as

fine a man, and seemed even proud of his choice: and
that she attracted the respects of the persons of rank
present, and had the blessings of the poor. — The
relater of the story told me all this with transport."

The novel, of which the above letter supplies the
outline, was published in November 1740, in two
volumes, and its publishers were, of course, Messrs.
Rivington and Osborn. After the fashion of Defoe,
its contents were summarised with much particularity
on its title-page, which ran as follows: — PAMELA: *or,*
Virtue Rewarded. In a Series of Familiar Letters from a
beautiful Young Damsel, to her Parents. Now first pub-
lished in order to cultivate the Principles of Virtue and
Religion in the Minds of the Youth of both Sexes. A
Narrative which has its Foundation in Truth and Nature;
and at the same time that it agreeably entertains, by a
Variety of curious *and* affecting *Incidents, is intirely*
divested of all those Images, which, in too many Pieces cal-
culated for Amusement only, tend to inflame *the Minds*
they should instruct. Like many other books destined
to popularity, *Pamela* seems to have found its public
before the reviewers had time to recommend it. There
is no notice of it in the December number of the
Gentleman's Magazine; but in the number for January
1741 (where the model Letter-writer is reviewed), at
the end of the Register of Books, comes the following
announcement: — "Several Encomiums on a series of
Familiar Letters, publish'd but last Month, entitled
PAMELA or *Virtue rewarded,* came too late for this
Magazine, and we believe there will be little Occasion
for inserting them in our next; because a Second
Edition will then come out to supply the Demands
in the Country, it being judged in Town as great a

Sign of Want of Curiosity not to have read *Pamela*, as not to have seen the *French* and *Italian* Dancers." [1] A second edition accordingly appeared in February, a third in March, a fourth in May, and the book was received on all sides with acclamation. At public places (Mrs. Barbauld says Ranelagh, but in 1741 Ranelagh was not in existence), fine ladies held Mr. Rivington's *duodecimos* up to one another to show they had got the work of which every one was talking. Dr. Benjamin Slocock of St. Saviour's, Southwark, who, apparently owing to a slip of Jeffrey's, has for many years been confused with Sherlock, openly recommended it from the pulpit; Mr. Pope is reported to have said that it " would do more good than many volumes of sermons " (an utterance which may have been just as much intended to condemn the cloth as to praise *Pamela*); and finally, at Slough, where the local blacksmith read the story to the villagers by the forge fire, his audience was so transported by the eventual triumph and marriage of the heroine, that they insisted on ringing the church bells. The only

---

[1] The particular French Dancers intended were probably Mons. Desnoyers, the ridiculed of Hogarth, and the popular Mme. Chateauneuf, whose non-appearance early in 1740, after repeated announcement, brought about the wrecking of Drury Lane. The Italians were those favourites of Frederick, Prince of Wales, Signor and Signora Fausan, who, at this date, were delighting the same theatre with *Les Jardiniers Suédois*, *Les Matelotes*, *Les Sabotiers*, and other " comic dances " and ballets. These came between the Acts of the Play of the evening. *Le Boufon* (*sic*), for example, was given, on 8th January 1741, after Act ii. of *As You Like It*. Richardson, perhaps, referred to these performances when, in the *Familiar Letters*, p. 236, he spoke of the Harlequinery which followed *Hamlet*.

jarring note we have detected in the general applause
is contained in an anonymous *Lettre sur Pamela*
(Londres, 1742) prompted by Prévost's translation,
and even this, a year later, confirms the extraordinary
popularity of the book, which the writer styles the
"*meuble à la mode.*" "*Personne,*" he says, "*n'en parle
avantageusement, mais tout le monde le lit.*"

All this shows unmistakably that *Pamela* — to use
a modern colloquialism — had "caught on." For this
there were several reasons. In the first place, it had
arrived in an exceptionally unfruitful period of English
Literature. Of its own class, nothing had appeared
in 1740 save *The Unfortunate Princess* of Mrs. Eliza
Haywood; while biography was represented by
Cibber's *Apology ;* the drama by Lillo's *Elmeric ;* and
poetry by such minor works as Somerville's *Hobbinol,*
Dyer's *Ruins of Rome,* and that *Deity* of Samuel Boyse,
which Fielding had commended in the *Champion.*
None of these could be described as epoch-making
productions. Then *Pamela* had the recommendation,
notwithstanding a name borrowed from Sidney's
Arcadia, of being absolutely unlike the "vast French
Romances" of D'Urfé and that "grave and virtuous
virgin," Madeleine de Scudéry — romances over which
the fine folks of George the Second were beginning to
yawn unfeignedly. It gave the ultimate go-by to the
stilt-and-buskin style of *Cassandra,* and *Pharamond,*
and *Cleopatra,* and the *Grand Cyrus ;* and it shovelled
ruthlessly into Ariosto's limbo all the mouthing
Oroondates and Ambriomers and Ariobarsanes and
other "most illustrious personages of both sexes," of
whose "history, travels, and transactions" readers like
honest Thomas Gent had been wont to hold ceaseless

discussion, and "find no end, in wand'ring mazes lost."

Nor were these the only, or the most important, advantages of Richardson's book. As the Slough incident shows, it appealed to the humbler reader as well as to the person of quality; it bridged over the then more widely-trenched breach between rich and poor; for who could say that a servant-girl who played her cards as cleverly as Pamela Andrews might not obtain a like reward? Then its professed moral purpose — a new thing in a novel — was a further feature in its favour. A work of imagination which could be seriously commended from a city pulpit, might certainly be safely studied by many who would have scrupulously avoided "those Pieces calculated for Amusement only," to which its title-page made shuddering reference. Published as it was "to culti-vate the Principles of Virtue and Religion in the Minds of the Youth of both Sexes," it might be read as securely as the *Practice of Piety* or the *Whole Duty of Man*. But more than these things, — more even than its unconventional freshness, its appearance in a "dead season" of letters, its appeal to a new audience, and its proclamation of a mission, — was the indisputable fact that it was itself a new thing. It dealt, not with people who had never lived and never could live; but with people who did live, and were then alive. It made them speak as they would have spoken, and what was more, it showed them thinking as they would have thought in their station of life. It entered into the minds of the characters described, and unsealed the springs of their laughter and their tears — especially of their tears. It was — we repeat

— a new thing, destined, as its author foresaw, to inaugurate "a new Species of Writing," — the Novel of sentimental Analysis.

To what extent, if at all, Richardson was indebted to preceding writers may be reserved for discussion at a later stage of this chapter. Turning now to *Pamela* itself, with full remembrance of the position claimed for it in the preceding paragraph, it is difficult to regard it in quite the same way as the readers of 1740. We cannot take the same view of Pamela's Virtue, or Pamela's Reward. To our modern ideas, she is much too clever for an *ingénue*. She is only fifteen; but she is as sharp as a needle. In her first letters, she quotes Hamlet, and she knows all about the story of Lucretia. What Richardson calls her "innocent stratagems to escape the snares laid for her virtue" have all the shrewdness of forethought, and from the first she has her eye on the main chance. We could perhaps forgive her for admiring her master; but, in the circumstances which ensue, it is impossible to forgive her for becoming his wife. No one has put this better than Mrs. Barbauld; and it is useless to go about in order to say what she has said sufficiently once for all. "The moral of this piece is more dubious than, in his life-time, the author's friends were willing to allow. So long as Pamela is solely occupied in schemes to escape from her persecutor, her virtuous resistance obtains our unqualified approbation; but from the moment she begins to entertain hopes of marrying him [a grada-tion, it may be noted parenthetically, which is drawn with extraordinary subtlety] we admire her guarded prudence, rather than her purity of mind. She has

an end in view, an interested end, and we can only
consider her as the conscious possessor of a treasure,
which she is wisely resolved not to part with but for
its just price."[1] In other words, when she reveals herself definitely as the " young politician " which one
of her satirists affirmed her to be, we are beyond the
blandishments of her red and white, her round-eared
caps, her russet gown, her really artless impulses and
her genuine good qualities, as well as all the meekness,
the humility, the charity, the piety, and so forth, which,
at the conclusion of her story, her creator thoughtfully invites us to admire. He further begs us to take
note of " her grateful heart," which, as manifested in
her extreme subservience to the " kind Gentleman,"
the " dear Master," who, having failed to ruin her,
has, to gain his sensual ends, raised her by marriage
to his own rank, produces a most unpleasant effect.
But after all, it is Richardson himself who is most
responsible for this, and we have no doubt that
he knew her intimately. Still he professed to be
drawing a pattern as well as a character, and his
heroine only embodies his views of the fitting attitude
to be observed in her peculiar circumstances. This
being so, one sighs to think of the impetus which his
unquestionable genius must have given to sickly sentiment, sham delicacy, and, as regards deference to rank
and riches, absolute snobbishness, by his admixture of
those things in the composition of Pamela Andrews.

Pamela is nevertheless the chief character of the
story, — the most convincing, the best realised. Of the
two Mr. B.'s, — for we cannot consent to regard them
as one — Mr. B., the rake, comes out of the play-book;
Mr. B., the reformed, out of the copy-book. Neither

of them can be said to be particularly interesting, or to be drawn from the life, although the author (as we shall see hereafter) professed to have some one in his eye. Lady Davers, his sister, again, is probably a fancy picture rather than a study. It is, of course, possible that a termagant of quality might behave as atrociously as she is made to do; and, according to Mrs. Barbauld, Richardson found flatterers ready to assure him of the fidelity of the portrait. Mrs. Jervis, the Bedfordshire housekeeper, Mr. Longman, the steward, and Pamela's parents, are all minutely depicted, but would be more interesting for a few humorous touches. Colbrand, the Swiss valet, and Mrs. Jewkes — Mrs. Jewkes, in particular — seem copied from Hogarth, and have a certain coarse vigour; but those who care to see how much such presentments gain by a burlesque treatment will do well to contrast them with the Mrs. Slipslop and Parson Trulliber of Richardson's rival. When we are told that Parson Trulliber's " Shadow ascended very near as far in height, when he lay on his Back, as when he stood on his Legs," we smile at an exaggeration which we are not expected to take literally; when Richardson tells us, in cold blood, through Pamela, that Mrs. Jewkes is as " thick as she is long," we feel that, in endeavouring to make wickedness ugly, probability has been violently strained. One of the notable characteristics of the book is its absence of landscape. The lonely house in Lincolnshire, with its carp-pond and its elms and pines, and the Bedfordshire mansion, with its canal and fountain and cascade, under the pen of a modern, would have been as pretty as a background by Mr. Marcus Stone. But *Pamela* has little description of any kind, the exception being that the author, like many another feminine man, seems to take a special pleasure in the catalogue of feminine costume, and can scarcely have omitted any detail, for example, of the "neat homespun Suit of Cloaths" which his heroine prepares when she is going home, nor of the silvered silk and diamonds in which she arrays herself when, after marriage, she repairs to the village church. It is in connection with the first that occurs one of those minute touches which show how carefully Richardson had studied the sex. "Then," says the heroine, " I bought of a Pedlar, two pretty enough round-ear'd Caps, a little Straw Hat, and a Pair of knit Mittens, turn'd up with white Calicoe; and two Pair of ordinary blue Worsted Hose, that make a smartish Appearance, with white Clocks, I'll assure you; and two Yards of black Ribbon for my Shift Sleeves; and to serve as a Necklace; *and when I had 'em all come home, I went and look'd upon them once in two Hours, for two Days together.*"

In the *Journal of a Voyage to Lisbon*, Fielding refers to the "conduct of authors, who often fill a whole sheet with their own praises, to which they sometimes set their own real names, and sometimes a fictitious one." This is a palpable reference to Richardson, who, in his character of Editor, prefixed to the first edition of *Pamela*, by way of Preface, a highly laudatory account of the contents of that work, supporting it by two equally laudatory letters to himself; while in the second edition, he added an " Introduction" of twenty-four pages, made up from other flattering communications which he had received in the interim. Even his friends, it is said, blamed him for this. One anony-mous clerical writer, whose protest is preserved at

South Kensington, probably went far beyond the
language of friendship. "You were bewitched," he
writes to John Osborn the bookseller, "to Print that
bad stuff in the Introduction [to the second edition],
for it has made enemies: As the Writer indeed calls us
all Fools, and of coarse discernment, 'tis a Requital to
your readers. He is too full of himself, and too gross
in his Praises of the Author, tho' I confess he deserves
much: but I believe has done himself no good in
accepting of such greasy Compliments. He wou'd do
well to alter it, and make it shorter." Richardson's
defence of the first "impudent Preface," as he himself
styles it, is contained in the letter to Aaron Hill, from
which we have already borrowed. Two of his female
friends, he says, gave him prefaces for *Pamela*, which
"were much too long and circumstantial," so he resolved on writing one himself, "and knowing that the
judgments of nine parts in ten of readers were but in
hanging sleeves, struck a bold stroke in the preface
you see, having the umbrage of the editor's character
to screen myself behind. — And thus, Sir, all is out."
Not entirely, for this explanation is scarcely satisfactory. At the same time, it must be remembered that
Richardson, as a printer, and compiler of "honest
dedications," had probably a good deal of experience
in the devious ways of prefaces, and may have conceived himself fully justified by precedent and practice
to do as he had done.

One of the results of the success of *Pamela* was the
inevitable sequel. This, which was published by Ward
and Chandler in September 1741, was entitled *Pamela's
Conduct in High Life*. Like the subsequent continuation
of *Tom Jones*,— *Tom Jones in his Married State*,—it is

without value, and deserves no consideration.   But it
had this effect, that it set Richardson upon continuing
Pamela himself, which he accordingly did, producing,
in the following December, two more volumes purporting to depict her "in her Exalted Condition," and
announced as "by the Author of the two first."   This
step, although, as we shall see in our next chapter, it
had some excuses of self-defence, could scarcely be
described as well-advised.   The interest of the first
volumes had perceptibly declined with the heroine's
marriage; and to prolong the narrative without fresh
complications was a manifest mistake.   Richardson,
moralist first and novelist afterwards, did not clearly
perceive this.   On the contrary, he put forth two dull
and platitudinous tomes with a maximum of instruction
and a minimum of incident, which Mrs. Barbauld justly
characterises as "less a continuation than the author's
defence of himself."   Among other things, Pamela
sends her letters and journals to the now reconciled
Lady Davers, who examines them critically with the
aid of a certain Lady Betty, while Mr. B. (whom the
author is artist enough to exhibit as not wholly reformed) gives a lengthy and "affecting relation" of his
past misdeeds.   This also is commented upon.   Then
Pamela herself turns censor, and examines Locke at
length.   She also records her sentiments upon Philips's
Distrest Mother, and Steele's *Tender Husband*.   Of all
this, it would be possible for a robust historian to
make rather cruel fun.   But it is idle to ridicule what
nobody now reads, and nobody read, even in Richardson's time, except his flatterers.   Indeed, it may be
suspected that the third and fourth volumes of
Pamela's authorised history are not unfrequently con-

fused with the spurious volumes entitled *Pamela's Conduct in High Life*.

As to the moral intention of *Pamela*, there can be no manner of doubt. But even when Richardson wrote the book, there were those who held that he had not religiously kept the promise of his title-page ; and the excellent Dr. Watts, to whom he sent the first volumes, replied, in a letter which has disappeared from the South Kensington Collection, that " the ladies complain they cannot read them without blushing." M. Prévost, too, if we understand him aright, considered it necessary in his translation to chasten or modify certain expressions which were calculated to wound the super-sensitive delicacy of French taste. On the other hand, the Reverend Edward Mangin, Richardson's editor, who wrote an edifying *Essay on Light Reading*, in which he is severe upon the works of Fielding and Smollett, has nothing but praise for the author of *Pamela*. We live in a free country ; and the same diversity of opinion is exhibited in the critics of the nineteenth century. Mrs. Oliphant, who regarded the sensation novel as " a resurrection of nastiness," thinks that the letters of Pamela, for all their pretence of promoting the cause of religion and virtue, " abound in nauseous details as explicit as the frankest of French novels," while the late Mr. William Forsyth, Q.C., a scrupulous critic, if there was ever such, is of opinion that, with the exception of one or two scenes, " they contain little that need offend modern delicacy." So much for difference of view ! But upon this topic, it may be well to hear Richardson himself, who, in his third volume, puts his defence into the lips of Mr. B.'s sister, Lady Davers. Pamela is curious, nay, anxious, to

know whether the letters describing certain of the
scenes of her life, and particularly those of "her two
grand Trials," have been submitted to the gentlemen
of Lady Davers's party. Lady Davers replies that
they have been so submitted; moreover, that she considers their recitals were necessary to the full intelligence of the story; and finally, in words that are
evidently intended for the gallery, that "it must be a
very unvirtuous Mind, that can form any other Ideas
from what you relate, than those of Terror and Pity
for you. Your Expressions are too delicate to give
the nicest Ear Offence, except at him [her brother,
Mr. B.]. — You paint no Scenes, but such as make his
Wickedness odious; and that Gentleman, much more
Lady, must have a very corrupt Heart, who could, from
such Circumstances of Distress, make any Reflections
but what should be to your Honour, and in Abhorrence
of such Actions." This is not a conclusive answer.
The charge against Richardson, if charge there be, is,
not so much that he has unduly strained the limits of
artistic presentment, but that, abnormally interested
in certain forms of wrong-doing, he has, in his descriptions, sometimes exhibited a more prurient preoccupation with undesirable details than is generally exhibited
by a moralist. But his taste in this respect improved
as he went on. As Mrs. Barbauld points out, his
second novel is far less objectionable than *Pamela*,
and his third not at all so.

Where even admirers make difficulties, it is manifest that the adversary will find matter to his hand.
The blemishes indicated by Dr. Watts were joyously
seized upon by those who resented not only the
teaching of *Pamela*, but the sanctimonious tone of its

precepts. In a volume entitled *The Virgin in Eden,*
and in another called *Pamela Censured,* opportunity was
promptly taken, sincerely or insincerely, to show that
the story, in spite of its pretensions, was not really
calculated to assist the cause of virtue. A third effort,
which purports to be from the pen of "Mr. Conny
Keyber" (a thin disguise of Colley Cibber), was entitled
*An Apology for the Life of Mrs. Shamela Andrews. In
which, the many notorious Falshoods and Misrepresenta-
tions of a Book called Pamela, are exposed and refuted;
and all the matchless Arts of that young Politician, set in
a just and true Light.* The contents, which were further
described as "Necessary to be had in all Families," may
be inferred from the title. Parson Tickletext presents
a copy of *Pamela* to Parson Oliver, as a new work
which has been praised by the clergy, and may be safely
given to his daughter or his servant. Parson Oliver,
who happens to reside in Mrs. B.'s neighbourhood,
rejoins by what he considers to be the true version of
her history, which is accompanied by what professes
to be her actual correspondence. This is both very
clever, and exceedingly gross. Pamela is shown to
be already hopelessly corrupt; and what the title calls
the "politician" element in her character is relentlessly
exposed. Summing up, Parson Oliver describes the
original *Pamela* as "a nonsensical ridiculous Book,"
which, so far from having "any moral Tendency," is
"by no means innocent." He also considers, among
other things, that it may have the effect, not only of
making young gentlemen marry their servants, but of
making servants desire to marry their masters, — the
latter being, in effect, no more than the point raised by
Scott in his admirable *Lives of the Novelists.* "It may

be questioned," says Sir Walter, " whether the example
is not as well calculated to encourage a spirit of rash
enterprise, as of virtuous resistance. . . . It may occur
to an humble maiden (and the case, we believe, is not
hypothetical) that to merit Pamela's reward, she must
go through Pamela's trials ; and that there can be no
great harm in affording some encouragement to the
assailant.   We need not add how dangerous this
experiment must be for both parties." [1]

A discussion has lately arisen as to the authorship
of this *Apology*, which has attracted to it more attention than it has hitherto received or deserves.   Miss
Thomson, who gives some account of the pamphlet is
disposed to attribute it to Fielding; and following
upon this, a writer who has recently prefaced a new
edition of Richardson's Works, speaks roundly of it as
Fielding's "famous parody," which is certainly to beg
the question.   Miss Thomson's chief reason for con-
necting the *Apology* with Fielding is, that, in *Shamela*,
" Mr. B." is already transformed into Mr. Booby, the
name given to him in *Joseph Andrews*. [2]   There are also,
besides the burlesque " Letters to the Editor " to which

---

[1] If we are to believe a review in the *Gentleman's Magazine*
for April 1754, the lesson of *Pamela* was not only learned but
taught below-stairs.   Among other things in the *Servant's Sure
Guide to Favour and Fortune* of that year, it is recorded that
John the coachman, by his discreet behaviour on the box,
attracted the notice of two maiden sisters of great fortune, one
of whom fell in love with him.   Further, that John, "*after
enquiring her character of many noble families* (the italics are
ours), consented to her proposal of marriage, and became a
great man."

[2] It may be noted that in some later editions of *Pamela*, an
endeavour has been made to neutralise this outrage by revealing
" Mr. B." as " Mr. Boo*th*by."

Miss Thomson refers, some minor touches which
certainly suggest Fielding's hand. The Mrs. Jewkes
of *Shamela* talks of her "Sect" like Mrs. Slipslop;[1] and
Shamela's own use of "Syllabub" for "Syllable," and
"Statue of Lamentations" for "Statute of Limitations,"
is quite in the manner of that estimable Waiting
Gentlewoman. It is curious, also, that a Parson Oliver
(of Motcombe) had been Fielding's first tutor; and that
Dodd, the publisher of *Shamela*, had published books
for Fielding. Finally, Richardson himself, writing to
"Mrs. Belfour" in 1749 (*Corr.* iv. 286), distinctly attributes *Shamela* to Fielding; and, in collecting material for this memoir, we have found confirmation of this
belief on his part. To a letter at South Kensington in
which *Shamela* is mentioned, Richardson has appended,
in the tremulous script of his old age: — "Written by
Mr. H. Fielding." All these things make for the
Fielding authorship. On the other hand, Mrs. Barbauld is absolutely silent on the question; Arthur
Murphy, who wrote Fielding's life, makes no reference
to it; and, as far as we can remember, there is no
mention of it in Fielding's works. If Fielding wrote
it, he must have been glad to forget it; and, in any
case, the mere assertion of Richardson, and even the
coincidences noted above, do not, in the absence of
further corroborative evidence, warrant any one in
describing the book as Fielding's "famous parody."

There is, however, one point in connection with
Shamela, which, if it tends somewhat to strengthen the
case against Fielding, appears also to indicate that he

---

[1] "Sect" for "sex" is, of course, as old as Falstaff. But
the point here is, that it is used in a book by Fielding and a
book which it is sought to attribute to Fielding.

did not associate the authorship of *Pamela* with
Richardson. Referring to the "Composer" of that
book, he makes Parson Oliver say : " Who that is,
though you so earnestly require of me, I shall leave
you to guess from the *Ciceronian* Eloquence, with which
the Work abounds ; and that excellent Knack of making
every Character amiable, which he lays his hands on "
(p. 6). " I have seen a *Piece of his Performance* (says
Parson Williams to Shamela), where the Person,
whose Life was written, could he have risen from
the Dead again, would not have even suspected he
had been aimed at, unless by the Title of the Book,
which was superscribed with his Name " (p. 52).
These are certainly not obvious references to Richardson. On the contrary, they seem rather to point
obscurely to Cibber, with whom Fielding had a long-
standing quarrel, and who, in his own *Apology for his
Life* (published a year before), a work which Fielding
attacked vigorously in the *Champion*, had described
the author of *Pasquin* as " a broken Wit," a " *Herculean*
Satyrist," and so forth, but without mentioning his
name. And if Fielding really associated Colley Cibber
with *Pamela*, it accounts in some measure for the
association of Shamela's *Apology* with " Conny Keyber"
— a surname he had already applied to Cibber in the
Author's Farce, ten years earlier.

Shamela appeared in April 1741, just after the third
edition of *Pamela* was issued; and it was not until
February 1742 that Fielding put forth what has a
better title to be described as his " famous parody,"
*The History of the Adventures of Joseph Andrews, and
his friend Mr. Abraham Adams.* By this time he was
certainly aware that Cibber was not the author of

Pamela, since, in his first chapter, he speaks distinctly
of the author of the life of Mr. Colley Cibber and
the author of the life of Mrs. Pamela Andrews as
different persons.   Fortunately, no uncertainty of
pedigree makes it needful to dwell here upon the
story of the work with which Fielding inaugurated
the Novel of Manners as opposed to the Novel of
Analysis.   Moreover, its connection with Richardson
is in reality but small.   Apart from the " lewd and ungenerous engraftment " (the words are Richardson's)
which makes Fielding's hero Pamela's brother, and,
it may be added, furnishes its least attractive scenes,
Joseph Andrews has not much to do with *Pamela*.   When
Parson Adams mades his appearance in Chapter iii.
the author's original purpose begins to be forgotten,
and after Chapter x. it is practically shelved, only
to be recalled at the end of the book for the sake of
coherence.   To Pamela herself, the references are few.
One usefully turns on the pronunciation of her name.
" They had a Daughter," says a pedlar at the end
of vol. ii., speaking of Goodman Andrews and his
wife, " of a very strange Name, *Paméla* or *Paméla;*
some pronounced it one way, and some the other."
Sidney, from whose *Arcadia* Richardson got it, made
it Paméla, and so did Pope in the Epistle he wrote
in 1712 to Teresa Blount: —

> " The Gods, to curse Paméla with her pray'rs,
>   Gave the gilt Coach and dappled Flanders Mares."

But Richardson, in Pamela's hymns, made it Paméla,
and his parasites persuaded him he was right.   " Mr.
Pope," wrote Aaron Hill, " has taught half the women
in England to pronounce it wrong."   Beyond the fact

that Parson Adams publicly rebuked Mr. and Mrs. Booby for laughing in church at Joseph's wedding, there are no further material references to *Pamela*, unless they can be held to be contained in Fielding's final words, which inform his readers that the hero will not be " prevailed on by any Booksellers, or their Authors, to make his Appearance in *High-Life*."

Of other works prompted by *Pamela*, it is not needful to make mention here, although they seem to have been numerous. Richardson himself, in a foot-note to one of the South Kensington Mss., says : — " The Publication of the History of Pamela gave Birth to no less than 16 Pieces, as Remarks, Imitations, Retailings of the Story, Pyracies, etc. etc." [1] But a brief word may be devoted to the adaptations for the stage. The first of these was *Pamela*, a comedy, played " *gratis* " in 1741 at Goodman's Fields. The author, one Dance, whose stage-name was James Love, was also an actor at Drury Lane. The piece had little merit; but it is interesting, because a character inter-polated in it, that of a fop named Jack Smatter, was

[1] One of the imitations, probably not included in the sixteen was Pamela in Wax Work, showing that " Fortunate Maid from the Lady's first taking her to her Marriage; also Mr. B. her Lady's Son, and several Passages after; with the Hard-ships she suffer'd in Lincolnshire, where her Master sent her, and the grand Appearance they made when they came back to Bedfordshire: The whole containing above a hundred Figures in Miniature, richly dress'd, suitable to their Characters, in Rooms and Gardens, as the Circumstances require, adorn'd with Fruit and Flowers, as natural as if growing. Price Sixpence each " (*Daily Advertiser*, 23 April 1745). Richardson must have visited this artless exhibition, which was just at his door, being " at the Corner of Shoe-Lane, facing Salisbury-Court, Fleet-Street."

written and acted by "a Gentleman," namely Garrick,
then beginning his triumphant career. He also wrote
the Prologue, which is included in his Poetical Works.
Another version of *Pamela* was prepared for the stage,
but never acted. In 1765 it again supplied the
material of the *Maid of the Mill*, a Comic Opera, which
had a considerable run, and was afterwards revived
successfully with additions by O'Keeffe. The author
was Isaac Bickerstaffe. In Italy *Pamela* was turned
into two plays, *Pamela Nubile* and *Pamela Maritata.*
In France, *Pamela; ou, La Vertu Mieux Éprouvée* by
Louis de Boissy, was acted at the Italiens in 1743;
and, in the same year, Nivelle de la Chaussée also
based a five-act play upon the book. *La Déroute des
Pamela*, a one-act Comedy by Godard Daucour, afterwards a farmer-general, owes its origin to the same
source. Finally, there is Voltaire's *Nanine; ou, le
Préjugé vaincu*, a pleasant little three-act piece in verse
suggested by Richardson through La Chaussée, and
produced at the Comédie Française in 1749.

On the other side of the Channel, as will be seen,
Richardson's first novel was the cause of considerable literary activity. It may therefore be well, in
terminating this chapter, to touch briefly upon the
recently-raised question of his alleged indebtedness
to Marivaux's *Vie de Marianne*. That there are super-
ficial affinities between Richardson and Marivaux may
at once be conceded. Both hit upon the novel of
analysis; and in this connection, no doubt, Marivaux
precedes Richardson. Their manners of writing were
also similar in some respects; and when Crébillon
the younger, describing Marivaux, affirms that his
characters not only say everything that they have

done, and everything that they have thought, but everything that they would have liked to think but did not, — he almost seems to be describing Richardson as well. But Marivaux's accomplished biographer, M. Gustave Larroumet, although admitting that there is no great similarity between the two heroines, goes much farther than this. Richardson, he affirms, " *a lu la Vie de Marianne ; il en emprunte l'idée et le caractère principal.*" Elsewhere he writes, "*tous les critiques du siècle dernier sont unanimes : la Vie de Marianne a inspiré Paméla et Clarisse Harlowe.*" Yet when we ask for the proofs, they are merely unsupported assertions. M. Larroumet does not even give them the honours of his text ; he puts them in a footnote. Diderot said so ; President Hénault said so ; Grimm said so ; Mme. du Boccage said that *Marianne* et *le Paysan Parvenu* were "*peut-être le modèle*" of Richardson's novels. What, however, are the facts of the case ? The first part of the *Vie de Marianne* was published at Paris in 1731 ; the second part in 1734 ; the third part not until 1735 ; the fourth, fifth, and sixth parts in 1736 ; and the seventh and eighth parts in 1737. Nothing more came out until 1741, when the book was left unfinished. An English translation of the first four parts appeared at London in June 1736 ; a second instalment in January 1737 ; and a third in April 1742, when *Pamela* had been published for more than a year. There is not, as far as we are aware, a particle of evidence that Richardson ever saw the earlier volumes of this version. In fact, the only discoverable reference he makes to Marivaux is contained in the postscript to *Clarissa,* and that occurs in a quotation from

E

a French critic (translated) taken from the *Gentleman's Magazine* for August 1749.   That he knew no French is demonstrable, and he could not therefore have studied Marivaux in the original.   Moreover, he was not in any sense a novel-reader; and in *Pamela*, the idea of which had been in his mind twenty years before he wrote it,[1] he aimed at a moral work rather than a story.   But what is still more to the point is, in the letter to Aaron Hill, quoted at the beginning of this chapter (to which M. Larroumet makes no reference), he has given so circumstantial and reasonable an account of the independent origin and development of the book, that it seems superfluous to go outside it in order to establish his obligation to a French author, however gifted, of whom, when he first sat down to write the *Familiar Letters* to which *Pamela* owed its birth, he had probably never even heard the name.

[1] See note 1 to p. 27.

CHAPTER III

The "Epistolary Correspondence" of Samuel Richardson may fairly be described, in vulgar parlance, as "a very large order." What remains of it — for it is incomplete even now — consists of no fewer than six vast folio volumes, of which the aspect alone is sufficient to appall the stoutest explorer. These six volumes comprise some eight hundred and fifty letters, or transcripts of letters, from Richardson and his friends, beginning in 1735, and extending to the year of his death. They are generally written — at least Richardson's are generally written — in a small hand, on quarto paper; and as they are written on both sides, are, when necessary, "in-let." The effect of this arrangement, when they are mounted side by side, is frequently to give four pages of minute script to a single leaf of the volume in which they are contained. In an unpublished letter to Aaron Hill of 29th Oct. 1746, Richardson gives his reason for thus packing his matter. " Did I not crowd my Lines into a little Compass of Paper, my Prolixity would seem more intolerable " — a device which he goes on to admit will not help him when his work reaches the press. As it is, he certainly contrives to get into a quarto page as many words as Swift could put into a corresponding page of the *Journal to Stella*. The difference is, that while Swift's line bristles with fact and illustration of the most various kind, Richardson's is often nothing but monotonous verbiage, and you may toil in the "immeasurable sand" of his sentences (one of his letters runs to five thousand words, which is a longish magazine article) without coming to anything which throws any light upon any aspect of his life or character with which you are not already sufficiently familiar.

Copious as is this collection, it would have been larger still had its writer become famous earlier. But previously to the composition of *Pamela*, he does not seem to have kept copies of his letters; and, as already stated, his correspondence with the gentleman who was "master of the epistolary style" had been long destroyed. Moreover, what must be regarded as the more interesting section of his letters belongs rather to the period which immediately preceded and followed the production of *Clarissa*, when he was in active communication with some of the cleverest and most stimulating of his lady admirers, — a period which belongs to a later chapter of this book. Mrs. Barbauld's account of the letters is as follows. During his declining years, she tells us, Richardson amused himself by selecting and arranging them, with a view to their eventual publication, either during his life-time or afterwards. They ultimately came into the possession of his daughter Anne, who survived (according to the *Dictionary of National Biography*) until December 1803, when they passed to Richardson's grandchildren, who sold them to Mr. (afterwards Sir) Richard Phillips of 71 St. Paul's Churchyard, the compiler of *A Million of Facts*, and the vegetarian publisher of Borrow's *Lavengro*. By Phillips, who is stated to have paid for them liberally, which must have been an unusual proceeding on his part, they were handed to Mrs. Barbauld to edit. In 1804 she published a selection from them in six volumes, preceded by a lengthy critical biography of considerable value, which, for a long time, and rightly, has been the chief source of information concerning Richardson. The original letters, which of course included a large number not printed by Mrs. Barbauld, were subsequently purchased by Mr. John Forster, by whom they were left, with his library, to the South Kensington Museum. But although, at the time of Mr. Forster's purchase, the collection included much unprinted material, it does not, as it now exists, comprise all the examples which Mrs. Barbauld selected. Probably in the interval between their ownership by Phillips and their ownership by Forster, letters were detached, and found their way into the hands of the autograph collector.

For example, the seeker at South Kensington will look vainly for one of the most important letters of the series, — that in which, under date of 1753, Richardson gave an account of his early life and career to Mr. Stinstra, the Dutch minister who translated *Clarissa*. From this Mrs. Barbauld makes copious extracts in her memoir; but, because she has done so, does not reprint it with the rest of the Stinstra correspondence in her fifth volume. Consequently nothing remains of it but the passages she has quoted — passages so illuminative that one cannot but wish for the remainder. Then there is — or rather there is not — the letter from Dr. Watts complaining instead of complimenting in the

matter of *Pamela*. This is duly enumerated in the
little manuscript index which Richardson had drawn
up of the correspondence relative to that work; but,
although it is in the index, it is not included in the
collection. There are several other gaps of a dis-
appointing character. In one or two cases, however,
the letter which has disappeared is printed by Mrs.
Barbauld, so no harm is done, provided she printed it
textually. Unhappily, after the old imperious fashion
of the old-time editor, she seems to have excised freely,
and many of the letters she has reproduced have been,
in technical phrase, considerably " cut." [1]

Among the *Pamela* correspondence is one letter she
has not reprinted, although it has obviously been
manipulated by Richardson with a view to publication.
The light it throws on the circumstances which led to
his ill-starred third and fourth volumes, is extremely
interesting, besides illustrating very significantly some
of the penalties of success in a thankless world. It is
addressed to James Leake of Bath, Richardson's
brother-in-law, and bears date August 1741. If this
date be correct, it must have been written before the
appearance of the spurious sequel to *Pamela* entitled
Pamela's Conduct in High Life, as that sequel came out
in September. Advertisements of *Pamela's Conduct*
had been published in the *Champion;* and Richardson, in response to a request for information, gives
Mr. Leake " a short Account of the Affair." Having

---

[1] As an instance of this, Hill's letter to Richardson of 17th
December 1740, which Richardson quotes in the introduction
to the second edition of *Pamela* (see *ante*, p. 37), there makes
three and a half closely printed pages. In Mrs. Barbauld (i.
53), it barely makes two, widely set.

heard, he says, that Chandler, the bookseller, had com-
missioned one Kelly, styling himself of the Temple
(this was, most probably, John Kelly of the *Universal
Spectator*), to continue *Pamela*, he remonstrated to one
of Kelly's friends.   This brought Chandler to him.
Chandler alleged he had understood that Richardson
was not going to continue *Pamela* himself.   Richardson
replied that he had certainly said so, though this was
in the belief that no one " would offer to meddle with
it, at least without consulting him ; " but that, if such
an attempt were made, rather than his " Plan should
be basely ravished out of his Hands," and his characters, in all probability, depreciated and degraded by
those who knew nothing of the story, or of the delicacy
required to continue it, he was resolved to complete it
himself.   He declared further that he should still
decline to do this, unless he was forced to it in self-
defence, but that if Messrs. Chandler and Kelly persisted in their enterprise, he must and would continue
Pamela, advertising against them as soon as they
published.

Upon this, according to the narrative, Chandler had
the effrontery to propose that Richardson should
combine forces with Kelly, and allow the combination
to be published with his name, — a proposition which
Richardson of course rejected with the contempt it
deserved.   It was next suggested that what Kelly had
already written (and been paid for) should be can-
celled, and that Richardson should continue the book
for Chandler.   To this Richardson very properly
replied that if he were forced to continue it at all, he
would suffer no one else to be concerned, and he commented strongly upon the baseness of the procedure,

and the "Hardship it was, that a Writer could not be
permitted to end his own Work, when and how he
pleased, without such scandalous Attempts of Ingraft-
ing upon his Plan." [1]　Upon this Chandler left him,
apparently convinced of the error of his ways, and
promising to consult his partner. He also promised
to communicate further with Richardson, which he did
not do. Kelly, however, seems to have sent what he
had written to the author of *Pamela*, in the fatuous
expectation that he must, upon inspection, approve it.
But Richardson, as was only to be anticipated, found
his purpose distorted and his personages caricatured.

It is needless, at this point, to pursue the story
with Richardson's own particularity; and we may
here take leave to summarise. Messrs. Chandler and
Kelly persisting, and moreover putting about the
report that he was not the real author of *Pamela*,
and could not therefore continue it, he thought himself compelled, notwithstanding the objection he felt
to second parts, and the mistake of pursuing a success
until the buyers were tired out, to set about volumes
three and four. He began towards the middle of
April, when he had ascertained that the rival work
was making rapid headway. His letter to Leake was
written, as we have said, in August, when he was
still busy with the work, and in recapitulating his
difficulties, he incidentally sketches his plan, which he
appears to have more fully thought out than one would
imagine from some of his statements upon other occasions. "It is no easy Task," he writes, "to one that

[1] This — it may be noted — was written previous to the "engraftment" of *Joseph Andrews*, which did not appear until
February 1742.

has so much Business upon his Hands, and so many
Avocations of different Sorts, and whose old Complaints in the Nervous way require that he should
sometimes run away from Business, and from himself,
if he could. Then, Sir, to write up this Work as it
ought, it is impossible it should be done in the Compass of one Volume. For her [Pamela's] Behaviour in
Married Life, her Correspondencies with her new and
more genteel Friends; her Conversations at Table and
elsewhere; her pregnant Circumstance, her Devotional
and Charitable Employments; her Defence of some
parts of her former Conduct; which will be objected
to her by Lady Davers, in the Friendly Correspondence
between them. Her Opinion of some of the genteeler
Diversions when in London, as the Masquerade, Opera,
Plays, etc. Her Notions of Education, her Friend-
ships, her relative Duties, her Family Oeconomy, and
20 other subjects as material ought to be touched
upon; and if it be done in a common Narrative
Manner, without those Reflexions and Observations
which she intermingles in the New Manner attempted
in the two first Volumes, it will be consider'd only as
a dry Collection of Morals and Sermonising Instructions that will be more beneficially to a Reader, found
in other Authors; and must neither Entertain or
Divert, as the former have done beyond my Expectation."

This quotation, if it does nothing else, shows clearly
that Richardson was more fully aware of the difficulties of the situation than might be imagined, and
that he was no mean critic of his own efforts. As
already related, *Pamela's Conduct in High Life* appeared
in September 1741, and Richardson's continuation

followed in December. On the 17th November in
the following year, he seems to have sent copies of
the four volumes to Warburton, having heard that
that great personage would be willing to assist him
with advice. A transcript of his letter, hitherto
unprinted, is in the Forster Collection. It humbly
invites Warburton's corrections — "if in his *unbending
Hours*, such a low Performance may obtain the Favour
of his Perusal "—in view of a future edition; and it
refers to the praise with which the first two volumes
had been honoured by "the first Genius of the Age,"
namely, Pope. Warburton replied in a friendly letter
of the 28th December, in which he said that he and
Pope, talking over the work "when the two last
volumes came out," had "agreed, that one excellent
subject of Pamela's letters in high life, would have
been to have passed her judgment, on first stepping
into it, on everything she saw there, just as simple
nature (and no one ever touched nature to the quick,
as it were, more surely and certainly than you)
dictated." "The follies and extravagancies of high
life"—he went on—"to one of Pamela's low station
and good sense would have appeared as absurd and
unaccountable as European polite vices and customs
to an Indian; " and he promised to develop his ideas
more at large when they next met. Whether he ever
did so, is not recorded. But seeing that Richardson's
continuation had been in existence for a twelvemonth,
the suggestion was certainly a little behind-hand, even
if Richardson had possessed the humour and knowledge of the world involved in such a virtual remodel-
ling of his plan. It was his practice to solicit advice
which, while it sometimes aided, oftener terribly

embarrassed him; and it is to be feared that this belated counsel of Pope and Warburton must be added to those other vexations which authorship brought upon a man already, as he told Mr. Leake, "oppressed with tremors."

But if there were vexations, there were also compensations. One of the admirers of *Pamela*, whom Mrs. Barbauld calls " Mr. Chetwynd," but who, upon inspection of his letter at South Kensington, turns out to be Swift's friend, Knightly Chetwoode, writes to some one who had lent him the first two volumes, to record his opinion (which anticipates Diderot's) that, " if all the Books in England were to be burnt, this Book, next the Bible, ought to be preserved." Then there is a mysterious letter from six anonymous ladies of Reading (one of them was certainly a Mrs. Lancelet) who have read the two first volumes and the continuation with equal pleasure. They beg Richardson to tell them, on his honour, whether the story is " real or feigned." They " have sworn themselves to Secrecy in this Affair." If the story be " feigned," they wish to know the name of the writer in order that their " Admiration may be turn'd upon the Author that could Paint ye Heinousness of Vice, and the Reward of Virtue, in such true Lights and Natural Colours." Richardson's matter-of-fact next-door neighbour, Mr. Vanderplank, to whom he must have shown this communication, seems to have doubted its genuineness.[1] Richardson's reply betrayed

[1] At the end of the joint letter comes: — " Lady Gainsborough and Lady Hazlerigg, we know, are exemplary Ladies, but can't find their Story in your Account." Mrs. Barbauld mentions that Pamela was popularly identified with both of

a like distrust.   It was copious, of course; asked for
particulars as to the names of his correspondents; the
nature of the oath by which they were bound, and so
forth.   He observed upon the improbability that six
Ladies could keep a secret, and there, after a brief
rejoinder from the ladies, the matter appears to have
ended.   Another of the miscellaneous pieces at South
Kensington is a long voluntary contribution from the
notorious "native of Formosa," George Psalmanazar,
offered for insertion in the second part of *Pamela*, and
detailing the charities of that lady to a poor family.
It was "coarsely written," and was naturally rejected
by Pamela's inventor.

Among Richardson's regular correspondents for the
period covered by this chapter, the more important are
Mrs. Pilkington, Dr. Young, and Aaron Hill.   Of these,
Hill is the earliest and most considerable; but it will
be courteous as well as convenient to take the lady
first.   Lœtitia van Lewen — such was her maiden name
— was the daughter of a man-midwife at Dublin, where
she was born in 1700.   At fifteen (Pamela's age), she
was married to one Matthew Pilkington, a clergyman
of literary tastes.   Dr. Delany, who had been her
father's college friend, introduced the young couple to
Swift, who seems to have been interested in them, and

these persons of quality, who were of humble origin; but she
apparently attaches no importance to the rumour.   It may
be noted, however, that Richardson's family favoured the claim
of Lady Gainsborough.   "The master of Pamela," says Patty
Richardson's husband, Mr. Bridgen, "was the father of the
present Earl of Gainsborough, who rewarded the inflexible virtue
of Elizabeth Chapman, his gamekeeper's daughter, by exalting
her to the rank of Countess; an elevation which she adorned
not less by her accomplishments than her virtues."

particularly attracted by the vivacity and cleverness of the "poor little child," who had been so prematurely wedded. He got a chaplainship for the husband, and introduced him to Pope and Gay, though he subsequently came to regard him (and rightly) as "a coxcomb and a knave." In June 1743, the date of Mrs. Pilkington's first printed letter to Richardson, Swift has lapsed into hopeless idiocy; and she herself was living in King Street, Westminster, apart from her husband, and terribly straitened for means. In the second volume of her *Memoirs* (pp. 238–239) she gives an account of a visit she paid to Richardson at Salisbury Court. Not having, from her Irish experiences, associated a printer with anything very exalted, she had paid no special attention to her costume, beyond being tidy. But she was surprised by the grandeur of the house, and the benevolence of the master. " He not only made me breakfast, but also dine with him, and his agreeable Wife and Children. After Dinner he called me into his Study, and shewed me an Order he had received to pay me twelve Guineas, which he immediately took out of his Escrutore, and put it into my Hand; but when I went to tell them over, I found I had fourteen, and supposing the Gentleman had made a Mistake, I was for returning two of them, but he, with a Sweetness and Modesty almost peculiar to himself, said, he hoped I would not take it ill, that he had presumed to add a Trifle to the Bounty of my Friend. I really was confounded, till, recollecting that I had read *Pamela*, and been told it was written by one Mr. *Richardson*, I asked him, whether he was not the Author of it? He said he was the Editor: I told him my Surprize was now over, as I found he had

only given to the incomparable *Pamela* the Virtues of
his own worthy Heart."

From the references in her first letter to money
advances made to her on behalf of Dr. Delany, and to
the fact that Richardson had " encreased her store by
his own charity," it would appear that this visit to
him must have taken place previously to June 1743.
From this time until her return to Ireland a few years
later, she must have been a constant trial to Richardson. Her other friend was Colley Cibber, who seems
to have been equally kind to her in spite of her
vagaries. "Common sense," he tells her in her ear,
" is no contemptible creature, notwithstanding you
have thought her too vulgar to be one of your maids
of honour." To Richardson she writes heart-rending
epistles from all sorts of picturesque addresses, such as
the "Blue Peruke, opposite Buckingham House, in the
Strand," and her subscriptions have all the ingenious
diversity of that equally impecunious epistolary artist,
Mr. Wilkins Micawber. "Your ever obliged, and most
truly acknowledging Servant, while this machine is
LŒTITIA" — is quite in the Micawber manner. Elsewhere the machine signs herself "TRISTITIA"; and elsewhere again, not with a name but a quotation, or rather
variation of one. "My name is lost, barebit, and gnawn,
by Slander's canker tooth" — a letter ends. Quotations,
chiefly from the play-books, abound in her communication. "Whatever I have read I remember," she says
upon one occasion, asking for Young's *Night Thoughts*,
which leads one to observe that, although she certainly
does remember a great deal, she has not accurately
recollected the quotation from *King Lear* to which
reference has just been made. She is always in diffi-

culties.   Her daughter comes to her "big with child,"
and her "saint-like methodist landlady" has turned
them both into the street; her "long-lost son," who
must have been the John Carteret Pilkington, who
edited the third volume of her *Memoirs*, arrives not
long after.[1]   Pending the procuring of employment for
him on the stage, he is despatched to Richardson, who
notes upon the maternal appeal: — "Ragged; destitute.
I gave him a suit of clothes.   He gave particular
orders to the tailor to make it fashionable to the
height of the mode."   The next we hear of him is
that he is going (like George Primrose) "abroad with
a young gentleman of fortune, the son of my most
intimate friend in Ireland."   His mother is got into
"a pretty decent room, at three pounds a year, in
Great White-lion-street, at the sign of the Dove, near
the Seven Dials," from which address she proposes to
issue a notification that "letters are written on any
subject (except the law) by Lœtitia Pilkington, price
one Shilling.   Also, petitions drawn at the same price."
But this must have failed, like the shops in the Strand
and St. James's Street, and the "stampt paper hats,"
which she could not go on with because she had no
materials, and had "only borrowed the stamps."   "All
my schemes are abortive," she says despairingly; and
it is no wonder she exhausted the patience of her
friends.   One of her funniest appeals to Richardson is
for "a few sheets of gilt paper, a few pens, and a stick
of sealing-wax," in order that she may write begging

---

[1] In 1760 he published his own "real Story," which has an
excellent portrait of his mother, mezzotinted by Richard Purcell
after Nathaniel Hone.   He is the hero of Goldsmith's white mice
incident (*European Magazine*, xxiv. 259–60).

letters to the nobility to raise enough to carry her back to what she elsewhere calls the "most unpindarique climate" of Ireland. Her last epistle to Richardson is dated 1749, and in the following year she died.

From Young there are not very many letters during this period. Mrs. Pilkington probably asked Richardson for the loan of the *Night Thoughts* because he published them. "Suppose," says Young in one of his later letters, — "in the title page of the *Night Thoughts*, you should say — *published by the author of Clarissa.* This is a trick to put it into more hands; I know it would have that effect." Young's communications are not very lively, and are preoccupied with his health. He is eloquent to his correspondent — with whom he compares complaints, and discusses the baleful effects of the equinox — upon the virtues of the Welwyn Springs, of steel, of the tar-water whose cheering but not inebriating cup Bishop Berkeley had celebrated two years earlier in the book afterwards known as *Siris.* "Tar by winter, and steel by summer, are the two champions sent forth by Providence to encounter, and subdue the spleen." But note, as regards the tar, "it must be *Norway* tar, of a *deep* brown, and pretty thin" — says Mr. Prior, whose book on the same subject, at the date of this letter, had just been issued. From another of the letters, dated July 1744, Young had been evidently visiting North End, and reading Miss Fielding. "I particularly insist that, when you go to North End, you let Cleopatra and Octavia know, that by their favour I was so happy, that in their company and so sweet a retirement, I thought, with Antony, the world well lost." Sarah

Fielding's *Lives of Cleopatra and Octavia* were not, however, printed by subscription until 1757, when she was
able in her "Introduction" to refer not only to the
"rural Innocence" of her deceased brother's *Joseph
Andrews*, but to the "inimitable Virtues of Sir *Charles
Grandison*." If Mrs. Barbauld be right in thinking
that Young refers to Miss Fielding's book, he must
therefore have read it in manuscript. Perhaps she was
trying to get Richardson to print it, — a task which was
eventually performed for Millar, Dodsley, and Richardson's brother-in-law, Leake of Bath. Richardson took
several copies of the book, and seems to have procured
other subscribers.

It has been already said that Aaron Hill is the most
voluminous of Richardson's correspondents at this
date. There are no manuscript letters from Mrs.
Pilkington and Dr. Young in the Forster Collection;
but, on the other hand, there are a good many of Hill's
besides those which Mrs. Barbauld has reproduced.
Hill's first letter is dated 1730; but it is probable that
this is a mistake, as the next letter is dated 1736. At
this time he was a man of fifty-three, whose career had
been sufficiently diversified. He had travelled; he
had written a poor *History of the Ottoman Empire;* he
had produced plays and poems; he had managed a
theatre; he had projected many things, including the
extracting of oil from beechnuts; he had even anticipated Oglethorpe in an attempt to colonise Georgia.
His house was in Petty France, where he had a pleasant
garden stretching to St. James's Park, and containing
one of the grottos of the period, to which his letters
make frequent reference. In 1738, soon after he began
to correspond with Richardson, he retired to Plaistow

F

in Essex, which, at that time, although flat and
marshy, was a pleasant, rural village "with roomy old
houses and large gardens," famous like Banstead Down
for its mutton, and offering every prospect of quiet
and seclusion.   His wife, to whom he had been much
attached, was dead, but he carried with him three
daughters, rejoicing in the names of Minerva (otherwise Minny), Astræa, and Urania, the last afterwards
married to a sublunary Mr. Johnson.   Hill's chief
object, besides literature, in retiring to Essex, was
another of the projects of which he had not yet been
cured.   As early as 1718, he had written an essay on
Grape Wines, and his latest idea was to establish
viticulture in England.   "I have been planting near a
hundred thousand French vines," he writes, "with
resolution next year to extend them over fifty acres of
vineyard."   It was not our climate, he held, but our
skill, that was at fault, "both as to managing the vines
in their growth, and their juice in its preparation."
One of the first results of his operations was that he
was promptly "surprised by an ague," and although
the following year he sent Richardson a bottle of his
vintage, it must be concluded that the enterprise was
not more successful than his earlier schemes.

A few weeks afterwards, on December 8, 1740,
Richardson sent him the first two volumes of *Pamela*,
for the acceptance of his daughters, but without
revealing the authorship.   Whether Hill had his
suspicions, it is not easy to say; but he wrote as if he
had none.   "Who could have dreamed he should find,
under the modest disguise of a novel, all the soul of
religion, good-breeding, discretion, good-nature, wit,
fancy, fine thought, and morality?   I have done

nothing but read it to others, and hear others again read it to me, ever since it came into my hands ; and I find I am likely to do nothing else . . . because, if I lay the book down, it comes after me. When it has dwelt all day long upon the ear, it takes possession, all night, of the fancy. It has witchcraft in every page of it ; but it is the witchcraft of passion and meaning." [1]

Astræa also wrote, for herself and Minerva, comparing the advent of *Pamela* to a breeze through an orange grove. On the 22nd Richardson replied, in a flutter of complacency, and, among other things, seems to have invited the corrections both of Hill and the young ladies. A good deal of Hill's next letter is occupied by an account of the effect of the book upon the precocious sensibilities of a six-year-old child named Harry Campbell, to whom the delighted author immediately forwards a present. Hill, however, was too shrewd, or too indolent to criticise his friend's style. He has endeavoured, he says, to go over it at one reading with the eye and the heart of a cynic, and at another with the vigilance of friendship, and has changed a word here and there. "Upon the word of a friend and a gentleman, I found it not possible to go farther, without defacing and unpardonably injuring beauties, which neither I, nor any man in the world, but their author, could supply, with others as sweet and as natural." As for Astræa and Minerva, they continue to be transported. After an effort to decoy Richardson to Plaistow, the whole family visited

---

[1] The letter from which this is extracted was one of the " greasy Compliments " which Richardson included in the " Introduction " to his second edition. (See *ante*, p. 38, and p. 54 *n*.)

Salisbury Court in July 1741, returning thence in a pleasant simmer of enthusiasm. In October, according to their father, the young ladies were in Surrey, still "preaching *Pamela*, and *Pamela's* author, with true apostolical attachment."

After this, there is a break in the correspondence of several months. Plaistow has turned out to be an "unlucky and ill-chosen place (most part of whose inhabitants we have seen buried)," says Hill; all the family have been laid up more or less seriously, and there are obscure references to domestic calamities. Richardson is genuinely sympathetic, and presses them to try change of air at North End. But they seem to have been compelled to stay on at Plaistow; and the further letters, until *Clarissa* is commenced, are mainly occupied with negotiations respecting Hill's poems and other productions, particularly the *Fanciad*, 1743, which at first, it appears, bore the extraordinary title of *Go to bed, Tom*. In some of these discussions, Richardson reveals a greater antipathy to Pope than might be anticipated, considering the commendation which the "first Genius of the Age" had bestowed upon *Pamela*. It is true that this was no new thing. He had been imprudent enough, he says, some dozen years before, in speaking to one of Pope's friends (it was Hooke of the *Roman History*) to prefer *Cooper's Hill* to *Windsor Forest*, *Alexander's Feast* to *St. Cecilia's Day*, and to express the opinion that Theobald was better qualified to edit Shakespeare than Pope, and though he had never known the latter poet personally, had reason to think he had offended him. He reverts to the subject in a later letter: — "I have bought Mr. Pope over so often, and his *Dunciad* so lately before his last

new-vampt one, that I am tir'd of the Extravagance;
and wonder every Body else is not. Especially, as
now by this, he confesses that his Abuse of his first
Hero, was for Abuse-sake, having no better Object for
his Abuse. I admire Mr. Pope's Genius, and his Versi-
fication: But forgive me, Sir, to say, I am scandaliz'd
for human Nature, and such Talents, sunk so low. Has
he no Invention, Sir, to be better employ'd about?
No Talents for worthier Subjects? Must all be personal Satire, or Imitation of others *Temples of Fame,
Alexander's Feasts, Cooper's Hills, Mac Flacknoes*? Yet
his *Essay on Man* convinces me that he can stand upon
his own Legs. But what must then be the Strength of
that Vanity and of that Ill-nature, that can sink such
Talents in a *Dunciad*, and its Scriblerus-Prolegomena-
Stuff?"

Hill's reply to this letter, which concluded with
another pressing invitation to North End, does not
appear to have been preserved. But his chequered
relations with Pope were now again interrupted.
Years before, upon a misreport of something which
Pope had said respecting his poem of the *Northern
Star*, Hill had attacked Pope. Being assured by Pope,
two years later, that he had been misinformed, Hill
"repented" fulsomely in a Preface to a poem entitled
The Creation. But a subsequent reference to Hill in
the Memoirs of Scriblerus, and a note in the *Dunciad*,
reopened the quarrel, and Hill rejoined by a satire
called the *Progress of Wit*, two lines of which —

" Unborn to cherish, sneakingly approves ;
    And wants the soul to spread the worth he loves " —

seem to have galled Pope considerably. But matters
were again patched up, with the result that for some

years to come a correspondence was maintained which
must have been intolerably tedious to the greater man.
It ceased in 1739 (when Hill retired to Plaistow),
probably, as Mr. Courthope suggests, because Pope
was "tired out with the length of his penance."
Hill's last letter contains a reference to Richardson,
whom he vindicates from any connection with the
matter of the *Gazetteers* which issued from his press, —
which matter at this date had given Pope much
annoyance. "As to Mr. R[ichardson] himself, (among
whose virtues I place it, that he knows and considers
you rightly,) there should be nothing imputed to the
printer, which is imposed *for*, not *by* him, on his
papers, but was never imposed on his mind. I am
very much mistaken in his character, or he is a plain-
hearted, sensible, and good-natured honest man. I
believe, when there is anything put in his presses,
with a view to such infamous slander as that which
you so justly despise, he himself is the only man
wounded; for I think there is an openness in his spirit,
that would even repel the profits of his business, when
they were to be the consequence of making war
upon excellence." How far this ingenious exculpation
proved consolatory to Pope we have no means of
knowing, this letter from Hill, as already stated,
closing their correspondence. But that the matter
rankled in Pope's memory is clear from a passage in
a letter to Lord Marchmont of the following year : —
"The very gazetteer is more innocent and better bred
[than 'our great men']. When he abuses the brave
or insults the dead he lays the fault another day upon
his *printer*." And in the "new-vampt" *Dunciad* of
1742, he inserted some lines which brought the

Gazetteers into the diving-match of the second book —
the same diving-match, in fact, in which Hill ambigu-
ously figures. According to Nichols, Richardson only
printed the *Daily Gazetteer* for 1738, and as Hill's letter to Pope is dated February 1739, it is just possible
that he may have "repelled the profit of his business"
on account of the scandalous character of the paper.

But whatever were Hill's feelings to Pope in February 1739, he must have revised them again by
the time of his death. "Mr. Pope," he writes, "as
you [Richardson] with equal keenness and propriety
express it, is *gone out.* . . . If anything was fine, or
truly powerful, in Mr. Pope, it was chiefly centered
in expression: and that rarely, when not grafted on
some other writer's preconceptions. . . . He had a
turn for verse, without a soul for poetry. He stuck
himself into his subjects, and his muse partook his
maladies; which, with a kind of peevish and vindictive
consciousness, maligned the healthy and the satisfied.
. . . But rest his memory in peace! It will very
rarely be disturbed by that time he himself is ashes!"
There is more to the same effect, which shows Hill
to have been but an indifferent prophet. From a
later unpublished letter, he must have had the arrogance to amend the *Essay on Man,* and send a copy
of it to Richardson, who (though he confesses to have
read but six pages) is of course "amaz'd at the
Obviousness as well as Justness, of the Corrections." He subsequently shows it to Mr. Speaker
Onslow, who judiciously observed that he thought
Mr. Hill undervalued his own Genius by giving the
public anything of his, which was not entirely his, —
a verdict which left Hill not wholly at ease. Another

of Hill's new or revived projects at this time was
a pamphlet entitled *Critical Reflexions on Propriety in
Writing: Separately regarding the Four Great Requisites
of Plan, Thought, Figure, and Expression.   Illustrated
by a frankly selected Number of Compar'd Examples in
the opposite Lights of Excellence and Error from the
Works of Mr. Alexander Pope, and other Late and still-
surviving celebrated English Authors.*   This pamphlet
was intended to develop the opinions above expressed
to Richardson, particularly in regard to Mr. Pope's
limitations, or, in Hill's words, " to leave it beyond
Will & Testament's Evasion that Mr. Pope knew
nothing, as to Plan and Thought, y^t merited the
name of Genius. In Figure and Expression, it has
shewn, he had some *Beauties,* equal to the Best in the
Best writers — And more *Faults,* and Lower, than
many of the Worst among the Bad ones."   Richardson
had the manuscript, but it was not published.   It is
interesting, however, to note that a good many years
earlier, at the time of his first reconciliation to Pope,
Hill had meditated a somewhat different publication.
" I have now," he tells Pope in January 1731, " almost
finished ' An Essay on Propriety and Impropriety, in
Design, Thought, and Expression, illustrated by
examples, in both kinds, from the writings of Mr.
Pope ' ; and, to convince you how much more pleasure
it gives me, to distinguish your lights, than your
shades, and that I am as willing as I ought to be, to
see and acknowledge my faults, I am ready, with all
my heart, to let it run thus, if it would otherwise
create the least pain in you: — ' An Essay on Propriety and Impropriety, etc., illustrated by examples of
the first from the writings of Mr. Pope, and of the last,

from those of the author.'" As Pope's editors observe,
this was an offer Pope could not possibly accept.
But as they also imply, it served to hang a future
criticism, amiable or otherwise, as the case might
demand, over Pope's head. Vain, and pompous, and
fulsome as Hill was, he was nevertheless critic enough
to say some very uncomfortable things; and this alone
is sufficient to account for the extraordinary tolerance
which, for the next few years, Pope seems to have
extended to him.

Hill died in 1750, continuing to write to the end.
The *Fanciad* being a failure, he made some further
progress with an Epic, begun years before, and entitled
Gideon; or, the Patriot. He also continued to project,
— his last enterprise being the making of potash. But
all his schemes, " crudely conceived " and " imperfectly
executed," were, like Mrs. Pilkington's, abortive. He
maintained his correspondence with Richardson, who
lent him money, and replied more or less effusively
to his fluent flatteries. The most interesting of the
remaining letters are those which relate to the forthcoming novel of *Clarissa*, concerning the progress of
which, about 1744, we begin to hear particulars.
Richardson has sent Hill two specimen chapters. He
is already nervously preoccupied with the possible
length of the book, and begs Hill to shorten if he
can. This Hill shrinks from doing, at first upon the
reasonable ground that it is impossible to compress
a part without seeing the whole, and then again upon
the ground that it cannot be compressed without loss.
" You have," he says in a passage which is, in some
sort, an apology for Richardson's manner, " formed
a style, as much your property as our respect for

what you write is, where verbosity becomes a virtue ; because, in pictures which you draw with such a skilful negligence, redundance but conveys resemblance ; and to contract the strokes, would be to spoil the likeness."

By July 1744 Richardson has sent him the entire design or compendium of the story, with which Hill is in raptures. "It is impossible, after the wonders you have shown in *Pamela*, to question your infallible success in this new, natural, attempt." From the next sentence, it would seem that Richardson had already roughed out the book. "You must give me leave to be astonished, when you tell me that you have finished it already." By October 1746 it is certainly completed, for Richardson, in a letter to Hill, has already been endeavouring to curtail its enormous bulk, and is sadly perplexed by a multitude of counsellors. A certain Dr. Hazlitt, who has read the whole to his wife in its longest form, is averse from parting with any limb of it or with any of the sentiments, and recommends him to do what the above-weight jockeys do at Newmarket, *i.e.* sweat whatever he takes away out of the whole. Mr. Cibber, on the other hand, who has also read it all, is for taking away entire branches, " some of which, however, he dislikes not." But these very branches Dr. Young will not have parted with ; and Dr. Hazlitt and his Lady, " who is a Woman of fine Sense," say ditto to Dr. Young. So Richardson, falling back upon a renewed offer of assistance which Hill has made, begs him to lend a hand in reducing the unmanageable mass, as the book is too long to send to press.

The result might have been predicted. In a few

weeks Hill sent back seven letters upon which he has worked, as a specimen of what he would do; and Richardson is alarmed. He begs him, however, to go on with the volume he has, so that, manipulated by Hill, it may serve as a model for the rest. Hill's alterations would cut away two-thirds of the book, and reduce it to three or even two volumes, a compression which is evidently more summary than he likes, as he doubts whether all he designed by it could be "answer'd in so short a compass without taking from it those simple, tho' diffuse Parts, which some like, and have (however unduly) complimented him upon, as making a new Species of Writing." "I am sure, Sir," he goes on, "you will not be displeased with me, if I rather alter by you, than verbally copy from you; and this the rather, as there are some Passages and Descriptions omitted, which have been approved by Persons of Judgment, who would be disappointed, if ever it be publish'd, not to find them." From all this it is plain that Richardson would have preferred not to accept Hill's version, but simply to use his work as suggestions for alteration by himself; and it is not perhaps surprising to find, by his next letter, that Hill has abandoned so thankless and laborious a task. It may be suspected that Richardson himself was not really sorry. "What contentions, what disputes have I involved myself in with my poor Clarissa," he writes to Young in November 1747, "through my own diffidence, and for want of a will! I wish I had never consulted anybody but Dr. Young, who so kindly vouchsafed me his ear, and sometimes his opinion." Young was probably one of his best critics; and it was to Young that he made the significant admission that he (Richardson) was "such a sorry pruner . . . that he was apt to add three pages for one he took away."

There are other references to *Clarissa*, both in the Hill correspondence, and the letters of Young and Mrs. Pilkington. But it will be most convenient to reserve these for the next chapter; and to conclude this one with a few biographical particulars. Between 1740 and 1748 nothing of moment seems to have happened to Richardson. In 1740 he printed "at the Expence of the Society for the Encouragement of Learning," of which mention has already been made, the first (and only published) volume of *The Negociations of Sir Thomas Roe in his Embassy to the Ottoman Porte, from the year* 1621 *to* 1628 *inclusive.* Richardson not only edited and prefaced this huge folio of over eight hundred pages; but he summarised its contents in a way that should surely entitle him to Goldsmith's praise of being "a dab at an index." His analysis occupies sixty double column folio pages, and each letter is abridged with a dexterity that would do honour to a Foreign Office *précis* writer. Hill, acknowledging a present of the great tome, says that he had discovered, with astonishment, that the "comprehensive and excellent index of heads had drawn everything out of the body" of the book; and for once his ready eulogy is not undeserved. Another work, also characterised by an elaborate index, is *Æsop's Fables*, with "Copper Cuts" and morals and reflections adapted from Sir Roger L'Estrange. As Richardson seems to have sent a copy of this to Harry Campbell, the little boy who had been so affected by *Pamela*, and as he specially refers to it in a footnote to Chapter xxix. of that book, where he quotes the fable of the Ants and the Grasshopper, there can be little doubt that the reforming and selecting of the fables, as he styles it, was done by himself. Two years later, in 1742, he issued in four vols. a new edition of Defoe's *Tour through Great Britain*, " The Third Edition. With very great Additions, Improvements, and Corrections." Of the books (in addition to Roe) printed by him during this period; and indeed of all the works printed by him (in addition to his own), not much is known. A collective edition of Young's *Night Thoughts* in two vols. certainly came from his press in 1749; and in 1757–58 he undoubtedly printed Mrs. Carter's translation of Epictetus.[1] He is also credited, in 1732, with a folio of Churchill's *Collection of Voyages*, and in 1739 with Maitland's *London*. But the triumph of the Richardsonian types must assuredly have been his part in the wonderful seven folio volumes of De Thou's *Historia sui Temporis*, 1733, by Buckley, than which, says Dibdin, no " finer edition of a valuable historian has ever seen the light." The book had several printers; but at the end of vol. ii. is " Londini: Imprimebat Samuel Richardson."

[1] " I do not think Mr. Richardson near so well this winter as he was last. Romances agree better with him than philosophy [*i.e.* the printing of Epictetus]." (Miss Talbot to Miss Carter, 20th December 1757.)

CHAPTER IV

THE dwarf-artist, Loggan, to whom we owe so many interesting sketches of the watering-places of the Eighteenth Century, has left one which usefully illustrates the life-story of Richardson at this period. The scene is The Pantiles at Tunbridge Wells, in the month of August 1748, when the public were supposed to be eagerly expecting the remainder of *Clarissa*, a second instalment of which had appeared in the preceding April. The open space in front of the Post Office is crowded with notabilities, whose names, according to the copy of the drawing given by Mrs. Barbauld in her third volume, Richardson himself has been obliging enough to insert below in his own hand-writing. Sailing up the centre in white, with an immense side-hoop, is Miss Elizabeth Chudleigh, " Maid of Honour to Her Royal Highness the Princess of Wales," and not yet the bigamous Duchess of Kingston and Bristol, though already married privately to Augustus Hervey. On her left is Mr. Richard Nash, Master of the Ceremonies at Bath; to her right, Mr Pitt, afterwards Earl of Chatham. In the middle foreground is a group including the Duchess of Norfolk, Lady Lincoln, Miss Peggy Banks, a " professional Beauty," who afterwards married Lord

Temple's brother, Henry Grenville, Mr. Speaker Onslow, Lord Powis, and Chesterfield's "respectable Hottentot," George Lyttelton. Garrick, a diminutive personage, is chatting with the famous *prima-donna*, Giulia Frasi; Colley Cibber is following, like a led-captain, at the heels of Lord Harcourt; *a* Doctor Johnson, whom Dr. Birkbeck Hill will not have to be *the* Doctor Johnson, is conversing deferentially with the Bishop of Salisbury, while Whiston of *Josephus* and the bombs —

> " (The longitude uncertain roams,
>   In spite of Whiston and his bombs) " —

together with the wives of some of those named, makes up the company. In the extreme left-hand corner is Loggan himself, talking to the woman of the Wells; and hastening out of the picture to the right, not far behind Whiston, is a compact little figure in a gray coat, grasping a stout cane in its right hand, and having the other buried in its bosom, whose identity is discreetly veiled in the reference as "Anonym." This is Mr. Samuel Richardson, of Salisbury Court, Fleet Street, and North End, Hammersmith, the celebrated author of *Clarissa*.

By great good luck, in a letter dated 2nd August 1748, — this very time, — Richardson has given a pen-sketch of himself which agreeably supplements Loggan's little portrait. It is addressed to his young friend, Miss Susannah Highmore, endeavouring to persuade her to come to Tunbridge Wells. After describing her " other old lover," Colley Cibber, as still " hunting after new faces," and referring to the dialogue sub-sequently published as *The lady's lecture*, which Colley has just written, he proceeds "to show her a still more grotesque figure," — himself. " A sly sinner, creeping along the very edges of the walks, getting behind benches : one hand in his bosom, the other held up to his chin, as if to keep it in its place : afraid of being seen, as a thief of detection. The people of fashion, if he happen to cross a walk (which he always does with precipitation) *unsmiling* their faces, as if they thought him in their way; and he as sensible of so being, stealing in and out of the bookseller's shop, as if he had one of their glass-cases under his coat. Come and see this odd figure ! You never *will* see him, unless *I* show him to you : and who knows when an opportunity for that may happen again at Tunbridge ? "

From another letter printed by Mrs. Barbauld, and addressed to his adopted daughter, Miss Westcomb, we get him in another mood. There is no date to this, but it was evidently written from Tunbridge Wells at this time, since it refers to Cibber's already mentioned dialogue as written, but not printed.[1] The waters have done him no good as yet, he tells Miss West-comb; and since dizziness was apparently one of their results, one wonders how they could possibly have benefited a sufferer from vertigo. His nerves are no better ; and the manners of the Wells were not attractive to a moralist, — especially to a moralist, however susceptible to feminine charm, who had rigorous views on conjugal claims and parental authority.

---

[1] It was published later in the year, in December, at the same time as the concluding volumes of *Clarissa*, and was entitled *The lady's lecture. A theatrical dialogue between Sir* Charles Easy *and his marriageable daughter*. By C. Cibber, Esq. London, 1748, pr. 1s.

There were very few pretty girls, he declared; and the married ladies behaved as if they were single. " Women are not what they were," says this observer. He did not join in the worship of the reigning Beauties, Miss Banks, Miss L. of Hackney, Miss Chudleigh, though of the last he speaks more tolerantly than most historians; and he makes mild fun of septuagenarian fribbles like Cibber who think themselves happy " if they can obtain the notice and familiarity of a fine woman." Once he finds the laureate " squatted on one of the benches, with a face more wrinkled than ordinary with disappointment. ' I thought,' said I, ' you were of the party at the tea-treats — Miss Chudleigh is gone into the tea-room.' — ' Pshaw !' said he, ' there is no coming at her, she is so surrounded by the *toupets*.' [1] — And I left him upon the fret. — But he was called to soon after; and in he flew, and his face shone again, and looked smooth."

In August 1748 Richardson was nearing sixty, and as the foregoing references to his health show plainly, a confirmed valetudinarian, suffering from some real and many fancied disorders promoted by his literary labours, and originating in the close application of a sedentary life. He had long been a vegetarian and water-drinker, and his health was probably not improved by the bleeding, etc., to which at certain periods of the year he was subjected by the barbarous

[1] Toupet was a famous wig-maker. *Cf*. Bramston's *Art of Politicks*, 1729, p. 10 : —

> " Think we that modern Words eternal are?
> TOUPET, and *Tompion, Cosins*, and *Colmar*
> Hereafter will be call'd by some plain Man,
> A *Wig*, a *Watch*, a *Pair of Stays*, a *Fan*."

G

medical treatment of the day.   He was liable to vague
" startings " and " paroxysms."   Crowds of any kind
he could not endure, for which reason he had left off
going to church.   His chief mode of exercise was walking, as he had never learned to ride except upon
the obsolete chamber-horse, a thorough-paced but
unprogressive form of equitation, which, at best, is
but a poor substitute for the saddle.   Some of his
letters would be ludicrous, were it not for their pitiable
exhibition of nervous prostration.   He tells Hill that
he has been reading his unpublished *Treatise upon
Acting*.   But he feels his whole frame so affected and
shaken by that author's " wonderful Description of the
Force of Acting, in the Passions of Joy, Sorrow, Fear,
Anger, etc.," that his frequent " Tremors and Startings" oblige him to suspend the perusal until by a
course of a newly tried " *Oak Tincture* " (recommended
by his correspondent) he can fortify his " relaxed,
unmuscled Muscles," and brace his " unbraced Nerves."
Had he known anything of Horace, he might, with
perfect fitness, have applied to Hill at this juncture
that *falsis terroribus implet,* with which, in the *Jacobite's
Journal*, the author of *Joseph Andrews* afterwards
complimented the moving author of *Clarissa.*

To *Clarissa* we now come.   It is sometimes stated
that the first four volumes were published in 1747,
and the last four in 1748.   Other authorities, on the
contrary, suppose the book to have been wholly issued
in 1748, *i.e.* four volumes in the spring, and four
in the autumn.   The mode of publication was
peculiar, and neither of these accounts is accurate.
There were in fact, in the first edition, not eight
volumes, but seven.   " I take the Liberty to join the

4 Vols. you have of *Clarissa*, by two more," says
Richardson to Hill in an unpublished letter of 7th
November 1748. "The Whole will make Seven;
that is, one more to attend these two. Eight
crouded into Seven, by a smaller Type. Ashamed as
I am of the Prolixity, I thought I owed the Public
Eight Vols. in Quantity for the Price of Seven"; and
he adds a later footnote to explain that the 12mo book
"was at first published in Seven Vols. [and] Afterwards
by deferred Restorations, made Eight as now." These
"deferred Restorations" were first effected in the
fourth, or larger print edition of 1751, the Preface
to which says — "It is proper to observe with regard
to the *present Edition* that it has been thought fit to
restore many Passages, and several Letters which were
omitted in the former merely for shortening-sake." [1]
Of the seven volumes constituting the first edition,
two were issued in November 1747; two more in
April 1748 (making "the 4 Vols. you have," above
referred to); and the remaining three, which, according to Mr. Urban's advertisement, "compleats the
whole," in December 1748. This is confirmed in
January 1749, by one of Richardson's correspondents,
"Mrs. Belfour," who, on the 11th of that month, has
read the last three volumes. These dates are of
interest as showing how great a strain Richardson
put upon his readers. What may be called the crucial

[1] Johnson, to whom Richardson had apparently sent a copy
of the edition of 1751, replies (9 Mar.), "I was . . . glad to
find that she [*Clarissa*] was now got above all fears of prolixity
and confident enough of success to supply whatever had been
hitherto suppressed. I never indeed found a hint of any such
defalcation, but I regretted it; for though the story is long,
every letter is short."

catastrophe does not take place until volume the fifth, so that they had to wait from April to December 1748 for those portions of the story to which the first four volumes had been but the leisurely and very deliberate introduction.

The student of to-day labours under no such dis-ability; and provided he possesses the requisite stamina, may, to use the figure of Colley Cibber, read to the finish "without drawing bit." The book, to quote further from the title-page, comprehends "The most Important Concerns of Private Life." And particularly it shows "The Distresses that may attend the Misconduct Both of Parents and Children in Relation to Marriage" — a sentence which might also describe both *The Newcomes* and *Aylmer's Field*. The story, which, notwithstanding its inordinate length, only occupies a period of eleven months, may be sum-marised as follows :—Miss Clarissa Harlowe, "a young Lady of Great Beauty and Merit" (we shall, as far as possible, employ Richardson's own description in his list of principal persons) has the misfortune not only to belong to an opulent family who are eaten up by love of money, but to have inherited as her own exclusive property the estate of her paternal grand-father. This gratuitous advantage exposes her to the bitter jealousy of her brother, James, and her elder sister, Arabella. Arabella is not beautiful; and her animosity to her sister is intensified by the fact that a certain brilliant and fascinating Robert Lovelace, who has been introduced into the family as her own suitor, so contrives matters as to transfer his attentions to her more attractive younger sister. Thereupon, Clarissa's two uncles, Antony and John,

announce their intention of leaving money to Clarissa
with the object of creating a family,—Lovelace also
being a person of means.   The effect of all this is to
increase the hatred to Clarissa of her brother and
sister, who determine to bring her alliance with Lovelace to naught.   Another suitor, one Roger Solmes,
an extremely contemptible and disagreeable candidate,
is brought forward, and presently the whole family is
drawn into a league against the heroine.   Difficulties
are increased by a duel between Lovelace and the
brother, James Harlowe.   Clarissa does not admire
Lovelace, whose past reputation is repugnant to her;
but the march of circumstances, and the persistent
way in which, both by himself and by her family,
he is kept before her mind, gradually result in her
taking — to say the least — an interest in him.   Under
the apprehension that she will be forced into an
alliance with the hateful Solmes, she is induced to
accept Lovelace's offer of protection, and, half-terrified
and half-consenting, is carried off by him.   Some of
the author's correspondents ventured to designate
this "a rash elopement"—a term to which he greatly
objected, since he had only intended to imply that
his heroine "was trick'd by Lovelace into his power
against her intention."[1]   But, having taken this step,
Lovelace's purpose undergoes a change; and however
honourable his intentions may have been in the past,
they now no longer tend in the direction of marriage.
His desire is only to gratify his inordinate vanity of
conquest, and to add Clarissa to the list of its victims.
Entangled henceforth in an inextricable network of
lies, intrigue, and deception, the poor girl, alienated

1 " Advertisement " to Clarissa's *Meditations*, etc., 1750, iii.

from her friends, and unsuspecting in her own goodness and purity, is decoyed into the company of some
of the most worthless of her sex, and finally betrayed
while under the influence of opiates.   After various
experiences in a spunging-house, and different hiding-
places, she finally settles down, broken-hearted, to die.
Her relations reject her; and though Lovelace, in his
intermittent moments of remorse, is willing to marry
her, her pride and inherent nobility of character make
such a solution out of the question. Serene in the consciousness of her innocence, "unviolated (as she says)
in her will," but mortally wounded, Clarissa gradually
fades away, and finally dies, leaving her suddenly-
awakened relatives distracted by remorse for her fate,
while Lovelace, who has richly deserved the gallows,
is compassionately killed in a duel by her cousin and
guardian, Colonel William Morden.

Such is the outline of this, in some respects repulsive, but in all respects remarkable, novel.   That
it should have been conceived by a middle-aged,
middle-class printer, whose first essay had been the
vulgar glorification of opportunism; — that the por-
trayer of the petty-souled Pamela should have preceded the creator of the "divine Clarissa," as it was
once the custom of her admirers to style her — are
problems to which it is idle to seek a solution.   But
the fact remains, that, in his second heroine, Richardson has drawn one of the noblest of women; and
that, notwithstanding his pretence of "no plan,"
he has constructed a story which, from beginning
to end, keeps her constantly before the reader in
the most skilful manner; disposes the subordinate
characters about her with the nicest discrimination;

and, in spite of an inveterate and constitutional diffuseness, manages to steer almost entirely clear of really irrelevant episode and digression. One smiles a little, and excusably, at certain traits in Clarissa's picture; at the details (probably studied from the Locke upon whom Pamela discourses so complacently) of her proficiency in "the four principal rules of arithmetic," at her knowledge of French, Italian, and the classics (in translations), at her systematic distribution of her time between music, drawing, and needlework, with its special allowance for sleep, meals, the visits of the clergy, and ministrations to the poor, for all these excellent qualities were indispensable to the stock-in-trade of the author's ideal woman, as he desired to exhibit her. But what he did not find in Locke and the rest was her better part, her purity and gentleness, her intellectual elevation, her dignity in distress, her resolute rectitude, her invincible determination not to stray one inch from her duty as she conceived it. This it is which makes the wonder of her being, — the marvel of her existence. "No Greek, no Italian, no English poet " — says Mrs. Oliphant, herself a novelist and a critic — " has painted such a figure in the great picture-gallery which is common to the world." We may continue the quotation, which is hard to better. "Neither ancient nor modern woman has ever stood before us thus pale and splendid in the shame which is not hers." . . . "Almost every other victim shrinks and burns with the stain of her own fault; and even Lucretia herself, if more awful, is less womanly, less tender, less sweet, than the maiden creature in whom nature and religion reassert their right after the first moment of frenzy; who calls for no vengeance, and

can accept no expiation, and dies smiling, of no ex-
ternal wound, but only by the deadly puncture of the
shame itself, making all other daggers unnecessary."
. . . "Not Desdemona, not Imogen, is of herself a
more tender creation. They are so much the more
fortunate that it is immortal verse that clothes them.
Clarissa, for her part, has but a garrulous and pottering
expositor, but in her own person she is divine."

For the betrayer of such a character, we cannot pretend to feel the interest which he inspired in
many of Richardson's contemporaries, and still, as it
seems, continues to inspire in certain modern critics.
He is much more constructed, or rather concocted,
than is Clarissa. He has to be witty, to be handsome,
to be daring, to be impudent and fascinating, to be
cold-blooded, to be supremely selfish and vain and
egotistical, not because Richardson had found these
qualities combined in one individual, but because they
are indispensable to the complex hero of his fable.
He must have been a rake, because a rake can always
be reformed; he must not be an infidel, because an
infidel would have frightened Clarissa away at once.
But Richardson, strange to say, although he had no
model for his heroine, save in his own "study of
imagination," pretends to have known some shadowy
prototype or prototypes of Robert Lovelace. Defending his delineation, in a letter to Hill of January 26,
1747, he says, "I must own, that I am a good deal
warped by the Character of a Gentleman I had in
my Eye, when I drew both him, and Mr. B. in
Pamela. The best of him for the latter; the worst
of him for Lovelace, made still worse by mingling
the worst of two other Characters, that were as well

known to me, of that Gentleman's Acquaintance. And this made me say in my last, that I aimed at an uncommon, altho' I supposed, a not quite unnatural Character." What he had said in his last, however, was not so conclusive. " I intend in him [Lovelace] a new Character, not confin'd to usual Rules: And something indeed New in each, or I should not have presum'd to scribble. . . . But this I must say, that I had not in my Aim [?] to write, after anything I ever read, or heard talk'd of; tho' I had in my eye something that I had seen years ago." It is, of course, possible, that the reference here may be to Wharton (though Wharton seems to be a most unlikely model for Mr. Booby); but as we have already explained in Chapter i., we do not think it likely that Wharton ever sat for Lovelace. If Richardson meant anything by his words, it could be no more than that he had chapter and verse for some of Lovelace's nefarious doings in real life; but Lovelace himself is an effort of his imagination, invented and modified and adjusted to meet the necessities not of realistic portraiture, but of a preconceived story and the evolution of a heroine's character. Richardson, in fact, was not a little put to it to make him at once sufficiently attractive and sufficiently detestable for the part he had to play. " Lovelace's character," he writes to Hill, 29th Oct. 1746, " I *intend* to be unamiable, as I hinted: I once read to a young Lady Part of his Character, and then his End ; and upon her pitying him, and wishing he had been rather made a Penitent, than to be killed, I made him still more and more odious, by his heighten'd Arrogance and Triumph, as well as by Vile Actions, leaving only some Qualities in him, laudable

enough to justify her first Liking." This was written a
full year before the publication of the earliest volumes
of the book.   In December 1747, when they had
appeared, the character is still being altered.   "My
Libertine," he tells Hill, "in the next Volume proves
to be so vile that I regretted the Necessity, as I may
call it, which urged me to put the two former to
Press."   All this seems to indicate that there was very
little study of real life in Lovelace; but that he grew
with the progress of the story in the heated brain of
his inventor, who furnished him with fresh qualities or
defects as they were required by the development of
the plot.   It is the triumph of the author's instinctive
art that, notwithstanding the improbabilities and in-
consistencies of the portrait, the picture is still decep-
tive.   Lovelace's crime is wholly indefensible and
unpardonable; but it is perhaps intelligible that his
dash and spirit, his wit, his impudence, his good looks
and his *airs de vainqueur* should have found him in-
dulgent apologists among some (Richardson indeed
says "most") of the author's lady friends.   "If I
was to die for it," writes one of these, "I cannot help
being fond of Lovelace.   A sad dog! why would you
make him so wicked, and yet so agreeable?"   It is but
fair to say that this was only at the fourth volume,
when he had not yet filled up the measure of his
iniquity.   After vol. v. her tone is changed.   "You
have drawn a villain above nature," she cries out.
"And you make that villian a sensible man, with many
good qualities, and you have declared him not an un-
believer."   Even in the infancy of the novel, and in
the throes of sentiment, the voice of the critic was
heard in the land.   For this, with other things, is very

much what modern critics say of what Aristotle would
have classed as that "improbable impossibility,"
Robert Lovelace.[1]

But while the writer (it is "Mrs. Belfour") touches
these anomalies, she says nothing about another matter
which has exercised many, and that is the apparent
impunity, with which, in spite of the most reckless
frankness in his written communications, Lovelace
carries out his flagitious proceedings. The first note
is sounded by Mrs. Barbauld, who thinks that in France
"his epistolary memoirs," and his gallantries (with
married women) might have passed muster; but that,
in England, he "would have been run through the
body, long before he had seen the face of Clarissa, or
Colonel Morden." Scott also expresses his surprise
that Clarissa did not invoke the assistance of a magis-
trate. "We will venture to say that Justice Fielding
would have afforded her [Clarissa] his most effectual
protection; and that if Tomlinson, the false Miss
Montague, or any other of Lovelace's agents, had
ventured to appear in the office [at Bow Street], they
would have been committed by his worship as old
acquaintances." The same ground is expanded by
the late H. D. Traill in an admirable article in the
Contemporary Review for October 1883. "The sufferings

---

[1] See Twining's Aristotle's *Treatise on Poetry*, 2nd ed., 1812,
i.,184, and note. "Such a being as *Caliban*, for example, is *impossible*. Yet Shakespeare has made the character *appear probable*;
not certainly, to *reason*, but to *imagination*: that is, *we make no
difficulty about the possibility* of it in *reading*. Is not the *Lovelace* of Richardson, in this view, more out of nature, more improbable, than the *Caliban* of Shakespeare? The latter is, at least,
consistent. I can *imagine* such a monster as Caliban: I never
could imagine such a man as Lovelace."

of Clarissa," he says, "are as those of an imprisoned
princess in a fairy-tale; the cruelty and power of
Lovelace is that of the giant ogre of the same order
of fable." Where was the law, he goes on to ask,
that enabled a libertine to keep in confinement a
young lady of condition, and himself meanwhile to go
about the world unmolested; and in another excellent dialogue in his *New Lucian* (" Fielding and
Richardson ") he makes Fielding say that " one of his
runners would have laid ' Captain ' Lovelace and his
lawless lieutenants by the heels in a very short time,"
— to which the Richardson of the colloquy has nothing
to reply. His own contemporaries had asked similar
questions. "It is even a doubt with me," says a
French critic of 1749 (translated in the *Gentleman's
Magazine* for June and August of that year, and
hailing from Amsterdam), " whether probability is
preserved in the detestable audacity of *Lovelace*."
. . . "Is this [enumerating his misdeeds] possible
in a country so jealous of its laws and its liberty ? "
. . . " An answer to these questions can only be
expected from a native of *England*." " Mr. Urban "
does answer in a footnote, and his answer is not convincing. " He [Lovelace] defied the laws of his country,
as many of his cast do.[1] . . . Are there not such men
in all nations ? in all governments ? Need we refer to
the public executions for crimes the most atrocious ? "
This, we shrewdly suspect, is Richardson's own defence,
as he refers to this very article in a " Postscript " to

[1] Lord Peterborough was said to have boasted, in his unpublished
Memoirs, that he had committed three capital crimes before he
was twenty. But then — as Swift says — he was " the ramblingest
lying rogue on earth.' "

Clarissa. "Laws grind the poor, and rich men rule the law," — he would probably have answered with Goldsmith. He had a servile conception of the privileges of rank, and he had a thoroughly democratic belief in the chartered wrong-doing of the upper classes. Moreover, for the needs of his story, he did not for a moment intend that Lovelace should be punished by the law. "There is no fear of being hanged for such a crime as this while we have money or friends." . . . "Besides, have we not been in danger before now, for worse facts?" These are Lovelace's own utterances to his bosom friend, John Belford, while sketching — very brilliantly, it must be owned, and out of pure sport — a fancy project for the abduction of Miss Howe and her mother.[1]

Belford and Miss Howe are the chief secondary characters of *Clarissa* in whom it is possible to take any interest. The lady is a very charming personage and correspondent, and it is to her that Clarissa (save when it is intercepted by Lovelace) addresses the chronicle of her misfortunes. Miss Howe is a contrast to her friend, to whom she is devoted. She has common sense, high spirits, and wit, which last she makes use of to triumph over her worthy and rather ordinary lover, Mr. Charles Hickman. Belford is a brother-rake to whom, in the words of the Preface, Lovelace periodically "communicates, in confidence, all the secret purposes of an intriguing head and

[1] The case of Lord Baltimore, to which Scott refers, presents certain curious affinities to that of Lovelace. Lord Baltimore was tried in 1768, twenty years after *Clarissa*, for a similar offence and acquitted. In his defence, while professing himself a man of pleasure, he warmly repudiated infidel opinions.

resolute heart." He is a collector and preserver of the correspondence — no light task. Gradually, he is reformed by the spectacle of Clarissa's beauty and purity, and in the end becomes her chief friend and protector. There are some five-and-thirty other characters; but they are merely subordinate, and exist mainly for the sake of piecing the story as disclosed by the above-named four. Of these again, the chief are the members of the Harlowe family, the sombre, despotic father, the weak mother, the envious brother and jealous sister, the sordid uncles, alike in their characteristics of inherited pigheadedness and congenital stupidity.

That *Clarissa* is Richardson's masterpiece, there can be no doubt. For *Pamela* is but an incondite production, which really ends in the second of its four volumes, while, in *Grandison*, though the manner is perfected, and the method matured, the movement of the story for the most part advances no more than a rocking-horse. But in *Clarissa* the simplicity of the central idea, the unhasting yet unresting evolution of the tragedy, and, above all, the extraordinary ability exhibited in the portraiture of the two leading personages, raise it immeasurably above either its forerunner or its successor. Richardson has been called an imaginative realist, by which we presume it is intended to convey that, as was said of Defoe, he lied like truth; and it is obvious that many of his ideas must represent abnormal accretions of invention around the minutest germs of experience. We have his own words, through Mrs. Barbauld, that, while professing to be natural, he had no personal knowledge of scenes corresponding to many that he has

described. But this would not prevent his hearing
about them, and we suspect that the little writing-
closet at North End must often have twittered with
pious horror at new narratives of outraged innocence,
or fresh disclosures of the vices of an aristocracy indicated respectfully by oral dashes and asterisks. Yet
even this, though it might explain the scenes at
Mrs. Sinclair's and the spunging-house, would not
throw any light upon the vivacity of the Howe abduction letter, or the travesty of the pseudo-Lady Betty
and "cousin Charlotte," or the inimitable scene in the
glove-shop at King's Street, Covent Garden. Of these,
and a hundred other passages, there is no solution but
the presence of that uninherited and incommunicable
quality which is Genius.

Although the publication of the three final volumes
of *Clarissa* was so long deferred, it seems that the
catastrophe was fully anticipated by many of the
author's readers. "I know not," he says in a letter
of 10th May 1748, after the issue of volumes three
and four, "whether it [the sale] has not suffer'd much
by the Catastrophe's being too much known and
talked of. I intend another Sort of Happiness
(founded on the Xn system) for my Heroine, than
that which was to depend upon the Will and Pleasure,
and uncertain Reformation and good Behaviour of a
Vile Libertine, to whom I could not think of giving
a Person of such Excellence. The sex give too much
Countenance to Rakes of this vile Cast for any one
to make such a Compliment to their Errors." "I
had never . . . designed," he says again, "that the
Catastrophe should be generally known. But one
Friend and another got the Ms. out of my Hands;

and some of them must have indiscreetly, tho' without any bad Intention, talked of it in all places." In a later letter (7th Nov.) just before the issue of the concluding volumes, he says, " These [advance copies] will show you, Sir, that I intend more than a Novel or Romance by this Piece; and that it is of the Tragic Kind : In short, that I thought my principal Character could not be rewarded by any Happiness short of the Heavenly. But how have I suffered by this from the Cavils of some, from the Prayers of others, from the Intreaties of many more, to make what is called a Happy Ending ! — Mr. Lyttelton, the late Mr. Thomson,[1] Mr. Cibber, and Mr. Fielding have been among these." That the author of *Joseph Andrews* had welcomed the first instalment of *Clarissa* in the *Jacobite's Journal*, is already known ; but it is interesting to find him among the advocates of "poetical justice." Cibber, however, is the only one of the four of whose views we have any definite particulars, and these are drawn from a letter written by Mrs. Pilkington to Richardson as far back as June 1745 — a very early date in the history of the book. She had related to Mr. Cibber, she says, "the catastrophe of the story " and the author's " truly religious and moral reason for it." Thereupon the tears stood in the eyes of the old comedian ; he raved theatrically ; he grew profane in his language. " He should no longer believe Providence, or eternal Wisdom, or Goodness governed the world, if merit, innocence, and beauty were to be so destroyed." Even Mrs. Pilkington herself did not approve the degradation of Clarissa. " Spare her virgin purity, dear Sir, spare it ! Consider, if this

---

[1] The poet of the *Seasons* died 27th August 1748.

wounds both Mr. Cibber and me (who neither of us set up for immaculate chastity), what must it do with those who possess that inestimable treasure ? "

This, as we have said, was written in 1745, more than two years before the publication of the two earliest volumes. But the most impassioned appeal to the author did not reach him until after volumes three and four had come out. A lady, writing under the name of "Mrs. Belfour," demanded of him in October 1748, whether it were true that the story would end tragically, and requested a reply in the *Whitehall Evening Post*, in which paper, according to Mrs. Barbauld, Richardson inserted a notice. Thereupon, this excitable inquirer addressed an impassioned letter to him, imploring him to alter his scheme, and make his "almost despairing readers half mad with joy." She pleaded not only for Clarissa; she pleaded for the reformation of Lovelace. "If you disappoint me, attend to my curse," she went on. "May the hatred of all the young, beautiful, and virtuous, for ever be your portion! and may your eyes never behold anything but age and deformity! may you meet with applause only from envious old maids, surly bachelors, and tyrannical parents! may you be doomed to the company of such! and after death, may their ugly souls haunt you! Now make Lovelace and Clarissa unhappy if you dare."

Richardson replied, defending his action with more decision and spirit than might have been expected in an author "affected by tremors." He had designed, he said, to combat and expose the pernicious doctrine that a reformed rake makes the best husband; and he justifies his "unhappy ending," as he afterwards

H

did in print, by a reference to the doctrines of Mr. Joseph Addison as expressed in the fortieth number of the *Spectator*.[1] Then he sends her vol. v. of the novel, which, as it contains the catastrophe, only makes matters worse. She still implores him to reconsider his plan. "It is too shocking and barbarous a story for publication." "I am as mad as the poor injured Clarissa," she says, in concluding her epistle; "and am afraid I cannot help hating you, if you alter not your scheme." Other letters follow. She does not care to see the remaining volumes; she cannot promise to read them; she is not at all anxious to know what becomes of all Clarissa's wicked relations. She wishes they had all been dead ten years ago. "I am indifferent now about every character in the book." When she does read them, as of course she does, she is terribly affected. "I verily believe I have shed a pint of tears, and my heart is still bursting, tho' they cease not to flow at this moment, nor will, I fear, for some time." "My spirits are strangely seized," she says again. "My sleep is disturbed; waking in the night, I burst into a passion of crying; so I did at breakfast this morning, and just now again." She is still unconvinced as to the ending of the book. She has lost an amusement she had set her heart upon, and now she must lock up the volumes, never more to be looked into. It might have been otherwise; it might have been that some one of them would for her life have "adorned her toilet." These

---

[1] "We shall defeat this great End [the raising of Commiseration and Terror in the Minds of the Audience], if we always make Virtue and Innocence happy and successful." — *Spectator*, 16th April 1711.

testimonies to Richardson's power " to raise and alarm
the Passions " come from a married woman of forty.
We shall hear more of her in the succeeding chapter
under her real name.

   In a Postscript to the novel Richardson deals with
the above objections, and with some others which had
been made to different parts of his heroine's story.
As regards a " fortunate ending," he elaborates his
arguments to " Mrs. Belfour," and justifies his action
by long quotations from Addison and Rapin with
regard to the practice of the ancients.   And he winds
up by saying that " if the temporary sufferings of the
Virtuous and the Good can be accounted for and
justified on Pagan principles, many more and infinitely
stronger reasons will occur to a Christian Reader in
behalf of what are called unhappy Catastrophes, from
a consideration of the doctrine of *future rewards ;* which
is every where strongly enforced in the History of
Clarissa."   Nevertheless, he contends that poetical
justice has on the whole been observed in his book,
since all the bad characters are exemplarily punished,
while the good ones are made signally happy, Clarissa
alone excepted, whom " Heaven *only* could reward." He
goes on to vindicate her from the charge of coldness ;
defends his making Lovelace a believer—notwithstanding his infamy, and extenuates the apparent insipidity of
Miss Howe's lover, Hickman.   He excuses his choice of
the Epistolary Style upon the plea that he had already
employed it with success in *Pamela,* and mistrusted
his talent for narrative.   And he defends, less successfully, " the Length of the piece " (it was the first and
second volumes in particular that were objected to)
by the contention that in order to give an air of

probability to a story of real life, minuteness and circumstantiality were unavoidable, in addition to which it had always been proposed that the story should be regarded as the mere vehicle of the instruction which was its real object. This brings us naturally to Johnson's well-known answer to Erskine when he complained that the author of *Clarissa* was very tedious. "Why, Sir," he said, "if you were to read Richardson for the story, your impatience would be so much fretted that you would hang yourself. But you must read him for the sentiment, and consider the story as only giving occasion to the sentiment."

The Postscript, it will be observed, makes no reference to certain other objections to what one of Richardson's foreign critics designates "the privilege, which he derives from the unbounded liberty of his country." The writer who has been already quoted from the *Gentleman's* of 1749,[1] and who, although he describes Richardson as "Mr. Robinson, a Bookseller," appears in other respects to be sagacious and well informed, complains, amid much praise, that the particulars of freedoms taken by Lovelace "exceed the bounds of decency." The scenes at Mrs. Sinclair's — he says — make him apprehend — an apprehension which, it is needless to say, proved in the sequel to be quite groundless — that in France *Clarissa* would share the fate of Corneille's tragedy of *Théodore*, which failed upon the stage, on account of a similar subject. These censures were answered by Mr. Urban, probably, as before suggested, upon the inspiration of Richardson himself. "The freedoms here objected to, seem to have been particularised to do justice to the virtue

[1] See *ante*, p. 92.

of *Clarissa*. . . . Whatever *coarseness of expression* the
great Corneille was guilty of in his *Théodore*, all such
seems to be avoided in *Clarissa*. A nice person of
the sex may not, moreover, be able to bear those
scenes in action, and on the stage, in presence of
a thousand witnesses, which she may not think
objectible in her closet." "Objectible " has certainly
a smack of the Richardsonian vocabulary. In what
is apparently a very rare Richardsonian pamphlet,
the *Answer to the Letter of a Very Reverend and Worthy
Gentleman*, observing upon the warmth of what is
known as the fire-plot scene in volume four, which
the writer had characterized as the "*only* exception-
able" scene in the entire book, Richardson defends
himself at great length. His defence is too detailed
to be summarised here, but its main points are the
obvious ones that his descriptions are everywhere
more restrained than those of his contemporaries, and
that in such a description as that excepted against,
and given by Lovelace himself, "the Lady's *personal*
as well as intellectual Beauties, and his avowed Passion
for her, characteristically . . . required that it should
be done with Warmth." Richardson, in short, shows
himself more of an artist and realist than the
moralist he professed to be. As an artist his defence
is unanswerable. But as a moralist, it is easy to see
that he might be accused (as Fielding was) of depicting
his hazardous situations with too manifest a gusto; and
there is something also in the suggestion of M. Texte
that, with Richardson as with Rousseau, "sensibility
verges upon sensuality." In any case, the objections
above referred to show that, notwithstanding the
favourite explanation of " other times, other manners,"

contemporary critics of Clarissa found very much the
same fault with her history as people do to-day.

The copy of the little pamphlet we have before us
has no title-page, so that it is not possible to say when
it was published.   But the date at the end of the
letter is 8th June 1749.   A year later, Messrs. Osborn,
Millar, Rivington, and Leake issued a small octavo
of 76 pages entitled *Meditations collected from the
Sacred Books; and adapted to the different Stages of a
deep Distress; gloriously surmounted by Patience, Piety
and Resignation.   Being those mentioned in the History
of Clarissa as drawn up for her own Use.*[1]   Opposite the
bastard-title is a sonnet to Richardson signed T. E.
(*i.e.* Thomas Edwards of the *Canons of Criticism*).   The
" Advertisement to the Reader " states that the Editor
of the History of *Clarissa* having transcribed, for the
use of some select friends, the Thirty-six Meditations
of the heroine, four only of which are inserted in the
history, was induced to give them to the public " as
serviceable to all such as labour under great afflictions
and disappointments."   It would also serve, it was
alleged, to accentuate the fact that *Clarissa* was not a
mere *Novel* or *Romance*, but a religious work. Whether
the Meditations which follow, and which are referred
to in a letter to Richardson from Mrs. Delany's sister,
Mrs. Dewes, of 24th September 1750, were originally
part of the unabridged book, is not clear; but Clarissa
certainly writes meditations and leaves them in her
Will to her friend Mrs. Norton, while the Advertisement further gives Belford's account of her from
Letter cxx.   The different exercises are from Job,

---

[1] For reference and access to this little-known book, the
writer is indebted to the kindness of Mr. H. Buxton Forman.

Ecclesiasticus, the Wisdom of Solomon, and the Psalms, and in a preface purporting to be prepared by herself she is said to have reaped great consolation from them. The book is necessarily one of which not much need be said in this place; but it enforces the sincerity of Richardson's attitude as a moralist, and what is perhaps more interesting still, illustrates the extraordinary way in which he identified, and continued to identify, himself with his characters. To a reader who should happen upon the little volume without further knowledge, it must certainly appear to bear all the marks of that genuineness which the author endeavoured to suggest.

Various attempts, even from the outset, appear to have been made to shorten *Clarissa*. Prévost's translation of 1753 was really an abridgment. Nine years later, after Prévost's death, Panckoucke the publisher invited Rousseau to make further reductions. But Rousseau, whose indolence was great, whose knowledge of English was *nil*, and who perhaps (as M. Texte suggests) was not particularly anxious to magnify further a rival author already sufficiently popular, put aside the task which, upon a hint of Villemain, was eventually performed by Jules Janin in 1846. M. Janin prefixed an interesting introduction to his work. The latest experiment in this kind is apparently that of M. Ernest Guillemot, who, in 1875, squeezed Clarissa's eight volumes into a pamphlet of some 150 pages. In English the first compressed edition was that by J. H. Emmert in the *Novelist*, 1792. In 1868 appeared two abbreviated editions, — one in the " Railway Library " by Mrs. Ward, the other by E. S. Dallas. Mr. Dallas, acting upon Scott's

opinion that Clarissa might have been a good deal
abridged at the beginning — an opinion which, from the
author's Postscript, was shared by his contemporaries
— has contrived to bring it within the limits of a
rather closely printed three-volume novel. It was also
condensed at New York in 1874. The late Edward
FitzGerald, an ardent Richardsonian, frequently refers
in his letters to the length of the book, which, shorn of
what he termed its " pedantry," by which presumably
he means its preachments, would in his opinion (and
favourite capitals) be " one of the great, original, Works
of the World." There was an impression that Fitz-
Gerald had actually treated it after his favourite fashion
by cutting out the surplusage, and binding up the
rest; but his editor, Mr. Aldis Wright, in a letter to
the *Athenæum* for 29th June 1901, stated that he
had failed to trace any effort of the kind.

But why abridge at all ? Why not leave the " large,
still, Book," as Tennyson called it, *intonsis capillis*, —
with locks unshorn of the shearer ? Any retrenchment
must be mutilation. And why mutilate to please the
modern reader who, when all is said and done, will
probably prefer a modern performance ? *Clarissa* is of
its author, and of its time; it can never be of us, or of
our time. Richardson was fully alive to his prolixity,
and fought doggedly against it. Consistently with his
aim and his purpose, he himself curtailed as much as
he thought his book would bear. Why not leave a
great artist who was true to his instincts in small
things to be also true to his instincts in great things ?
His genuine lovers will never be contented with a compressed *Clarissa ;* and for the much-considered " modern
reader " he must e'en be left to the fate which Johnson

foresaw for those who study their Richardson for the story and the story alone. At the same time, it may be permitted to doubt whether, in the present year of grace, he will ever find an admirer fervent enough to peruse him, like his " sincerely obliged " Miss Margaret Collier, four several times; still less to read *Clarissa*, like Mr. Edwards of Turrick, " at least once a year," in addition to *Pamela* and *Grandison*.

CHAPTER V

THE "lewd and ungenerous engraftment" on *Pamela* of Fielding's *Joseph Andrews* had naturally been a terrible thorn in Richardson's side. If to this be added that, rightly or wrongly, he also saw in him the anonymous author of *Shamela*, the offence must certainly have "smelt to heaven." Of late, however, Fielding had made some overtures towards an *amende honorable.* In the *Jacobite's Journal,* he had cordially praised the first two volumes of *Clarissa.* "Such Simplicity, such Manners, such deep Penetration into Nature; such Power to raise and alarm the Passions, few Writers, either ancient or modern, have been possessed of," — he had declared. And then he had made an apposite quotation from Horace,[1] which quotation (with a line or two more to show that he had consulted the original) Richardson subsequently inserted in his Postscript, and an admirer turned into the first quatrain of an introductory sonnet to Clarissa's history : —

> " O Master of the heart ! whose magic skill
> The close recesses of the soul can find,
> Can rouse, becalm, and terrify the mind,
> Now melt with pity, now with anguish thrill " ;

[1] " Pectus inaniter angit,
Irritat, mulcet, falsis terroribus implet
Ut magus." HOR. *Epp.* ii. i. 211-13.

and so forth. As we have seen, Fielding had also been
among the advocates of a " happy ending,"— which was
an additional testimony to his interest in the book.
But in February 1749 he unhappily sinned again, and
this time beyond the possibility of pardon. He published *Tom Jones*.

It is probable that the publication of *Tom Jones*
annoyed Richardson far more than the publication
either of *Shamela* or of *Joseph Andrews*. For these he
could always console himself by real or pretended
contempt, and by what, in many cases, was the genuine
sympathy of his friends. But with *Tom Jones*, Fielding
appeared as a definite rival in fiction, professing like
himself to administer a "new Province of Writing,"
and having a public of recognised and enthusiastic
supporters. The young ladies of her neighbourhood,
" Mrs. Belfour " told the sensitive author of *Clarissa*,
were for ever talking about their favourites as their
" Tom Joneses," and the gentlemen on their side had
their Sophias, one of them going so far as to give that
honoured name to his " Dutch mastiff puppy." In a
flutter of jealous apprehension, Richardson turned to
his sympathetic friends, Astræa and Minerva at
Plaistow. What did they think of this "coarse-titled"
book, with its " spurious brat " ? He had not read it
himself, — not he. But he evidently knew a good deal
about its contents. Astræa and Minerva took him
literally ; and gave a very business-like, and far too
favourable report of their impressions of Mr. Fielding's
performance. Indeed, upon the whole, they blessed
rather than cursed. They discovered in it " a double
Merit, both of Head, and *Heart*." They praised its
construction. They held that the events of the fable

"rewarded Sincerity, punished and exposed Hypoc-
risy, showed Pity and Benevolence in amiable Lights,
and Avarice and Brutality in very despicable ones."
This was too much for Richardson who, while still
declining to read the book, rejoined by criticising
plot, hero, and heroine with such energy as to draw
tears of vexation from the fine eyes of Minerva
and Astræa, who presently found themselves in the
discreditable predicament of having approved "a work
of *Evil Tendency*." Nevertheless they stood gallantly
by their guns, and still hoped, through their father,
that when their honoured friend at Fulham had time
to study *Tom Jones* for himself, he might detect "a
Thread of Moral meaning" in it. Richardson replied,
of course, — and at length. He referred to Fielding as
a "very indelicate, a very impetuous, an unyielding-
spirited Man." But he promised vaguely that he
would, if opportunity offered, "bestow a Reading" on
Tom Jones. Whether he eventually did so, it is difficult to decide. But in a letter to another correspondent,
dated January 1750 — a letter in which he continues
to harp on "the weak, the insipid, the Runaway, the
Inn-frequenting Sophia" and her "illegitimate Tom"
— he professes, as before, to speak on hearsay. Had
he been at leisure to examine *Tom Jones* (if, indeed, it
were possible to have leisure for such a task!), he
would no doubt be able "to do the Author impartial
Justice." Upon this point, perhaps, it may be per-
missible to entertain misgivings. But he must, at
least, have had his consolations. One Solomon Lowe,
the author of a "Critical Spelling Book," gravely
assured him that all Europe would ultimately ring
with *Clarissa*, "when a Cracker, that was some thous^d

hours a-composing,[1] will no longer be heard or talk't-of."
Mr. Lowe's letter is to be seen at South Kensington;
and Richardson has gravely endorsed it with his own
hand—" Cracker, T. Jones."

Of the correspondents to whom this chapter relates,
the majority are women. " My acquaintance," says
Richardson in one place, " lies chiefly among the
ladies; I care not who knows it." In the interval
between the publication of *Pamela* and the publication
of *Clarissa*, he had added a good many new friends of
the other sex to his list. The most voluminous of
these was the lady already referred to as " Mrs.
Belfour," of whom, and of whose real title, we shall
speak hereafter. Among the earlier, come three
names, with which Richardson and his rival are more
or less connected—those of Sarah Fielding, and the
two sisters, Jane and Margaret Collier. With Sarah
Fielding, and indeed with all the Miss Fieldings,
Richardson appears to have been on a friendly footing.
In his letter to Astræa and Minerva Hill he says, "I
love Four worthy Sisters of his [Fielding], with whom
I am well acquainted." As already pointed out, in
speaking of the Young correspondence, Sarah Fielding
must have been a visitor at North End as early as
1744, and in one of her own epistles, dated January
1749, she refers to the gratification it would have
afforded her to act as Richardson's secretary. " Pleasantly surprised should I have been, suddenly to have
found all my thoughts strengthened, and my words
flow into an easy and nervous style," she writes—
expressions which suggest that the accomplished
author of *David Simple* was not averse from exercising

[1] See *Tom Jones*, Bk. xi. Ch. i.

that form of flattery which Bacon defines as praising
a man for those things wherein "he is most Defective"
—as, for instance, he himself did when he commended
James I. for his slobbering elocution.   But it must be
owned that if his friends praised Richardson, he paid
them (like Garrick) in kind.   " I have just gone
thro'"—" re-perused " is the word elsewhere — " your
two vols. of Letters," he writes to Sarah Fielding in
December 1756.   [These were manifestly the *Familiar
Letters between the Principal Characters in David Simple*,
1747.]   " What a knowledge of the human heart !
Well might a critical judge of writing say, as he did
to me, that your late brother's knowledge of it was
not (fine writer as he was) comparable to yours.   His
was but as the knowledge of the outside of a clock-
work machine, while yours was that of all the finer
springs and movements of the inside."   Curiously
enough, this is very much the praise which, a dozen
years later, Johnson, no doubt the critical judge
referred to, gave to Richardson himself.   " There
was as great a difference between them [Richardson
and Fielding]," he said, " as between a man who knew
how a watch was made, and a man who could tell the
hour by looking on the dial-plate."   With her brother
on one side, and Richardson on the other, poor Miss
Fielding must have been sadly embarrassed.   For if
Richardson praised her, her brother, on his part, was
not behindhand.   He had written a friendly preface
to *David Simple;* and he had not only prefaced the
Familiar Letters, but, as Richardson should have known
if he read to the end of the second volume, had
written five of them himself, and those by no means
the least important.   And, of those which he had *not*

written, he had said that they contained "Touches of Nature" — "as fine, as he had ever met with in any of the Authors, who had made Human Nature their Subject." Thus we have the first two novelists of their age, and rivals to boot, combining to praise a third, whose work — to use an expressive phrase of Mr. Forster — must now be disinterred in order to be discussed.

Sarah Fielding, nevertheless, was by no means without ability. She was a scholar, in days when women-scholars were rarer; and, according to those who knew her later at Bath, much respected, both for her character and talents, though she must always have been in necessitous circumstances. This must also have been the case of her friends, the two Miss Colliers, the daughters of Arthur Collier, the metaphysician; and there are indications that they were all three indebted to Richardson for presents of money. Jane Collier was Sarah Fielding's collaborator in the "dramatic Fable" called "The Cry." The other sister, Margaret, a frequent sojourner at North End, was also the young lady who is said to have cut out in paper that profile of Fielding which is fabled to have served as a guide to Hogarth in drawing his friend's protrait from memory. She had lived with Fielding at Ealing, where she witnessed his will, and she was one of the little party which accompanied him to Lisbon. But her obligations to Richardson must have afterwards wholly overcome any gratitude which she may have owed to his rival. "I was sadly vexed," she writes in 1755 from Ryde, to which place, after her sister's death, she had retired, "at my first coming, at a report which had prevailed here, of my being the author of Mr. Fielding's last work, *The Voyage to Lisbon :* the reason which was given for supposing it mine, was to the last degree mortifying, viz. that it was so very bad a performance, and fell so far short of his other works, it must needs be the person *with him* who wrote it." In much the same strain writes another of Richardson's friends. " I have lately read over with much indignation Fielding's last piece, called his *Voyage to Lisbon.* That a man, who had led such a life as he had, should trifle in that manner when immediate death was before his eyes, is amazing. From this book I am confirmed in what his other works had fully persuaded me of, that with all his parade of pretences to virtuous and humane affections, the fellow had no heart. And so — his knell is knolled."

The writer of this precious piece of criticism was Thomas Edwards, a bachelor, and a barrister who never practised. Next to Young he was the most important of Richardson's male correspondents. He does not often give vent to such outbursts, and seems to have been usually what Mrs. Barbauld calls him, a " very good, pious, and kind-hearted man." He was the friend of Richard Owen Cambridge, Walpole's " Cambridge the Everything," of the parodist, Isaac Hawkins Browne, and of Mr. Speaker Onslow. Indeed, it may have been at Ember Court that he first made Richardson's acquaintance, for they were certainly there together. His first letter, from which it is clear that he has also been visiting at North End, is an acknowledgment of the " divine Clarissa," to whom he attributes an exaggerated effect upon the manners of the age. " I am not without hope that this excellent work has already had some influence on the town ; and cannot help thinking that the approbation with which I am told the tender scenes between Romeo and Juliet were received, above the humorous ones between Benedick and Beatrice, might be owing to impressions made by Clarissa, who has tamed and humanised hearts that before were not so very sensible. "[1] Richardson, of course, was delighted, and a correspondence ensued which lasted for several years, the quotation as to Fielding being taken from a letter of May 1755, whereas the words just given are from one of January 1749. Edwards was, in his way, a notable man ; and Miss Thomson is right in claiming for him a position among the pioneers of the romantic revival. He was a genuine lover of the older writers — of Shakespeare, of Milton, of Spenser in particular, who had set him upon writing sonnets, although he afterwards observed the Miltonic rule. Many of these performances, which Richardson wanted to print during Edwards's life-time, are included in the Introduction to Cambridge's *Works* of 1803. There are others in the second volume of Dodsley's *Collection*, and, as we have seen, he composed an introductory sonnet for Clarissa's *Meditations*. Moreover, a few years earlier, he had written a clever *Supplement to Warburton's Edition of Shakespeare*, later known as the *Canons of Criticism*, in

---

[1] In November 1748 *Much Ado about Nothing* had been acted at Drury Lane with Garrick as Benedick, and Mrs. Pritchard as Beatrice. It ran eight nights, and was followed by *Romeo and Juliet*, with Barry as Romeo and Mrs. Cibber as Juliet. This was played for nineteen nights. But it is to be feared that Barry's magnificent presence and Mrs. Cibber's beauty had more to do with its success than the publication of *Clarissa*.

which he exposed some of the Bishop's arrogant pretensions, — a pamphlet concerning which it has always
been held that it deserved more praise than Warburton's friend, Dr. Johnson, was inclined to allow to it.
Richardson, who fancied he had been snubbed by
Warburton, would have pressed Edwards to expose
Warburton further still in a rival edition of Pope.
But although Edwards, like his friend Cambridge, had
contributed minerals to Pope's Twickenham grotto, he
was not so thorough-going an admirer of the author of
the *Essay on Man* as to undertake this enterprise. His
real enthusiasm was reserved for the older writers ;
and his abilities were of that leisurely kind which
dabbles in philology and folklore, skirts the fringes
of a subject, and prefers to generalise about eclectic
editions and grumble at " vamping " publishers, rather
than to embark with resolution upon any definite task.
He visited North End frequently from his home at
Turrick, near Wendover in Bucks, making friends with
Richardson's little circle of " Muses and Graces," and
inspiring the younger members with his trick of
sonneteering. He died finally under Richardson's
roof in 1757.

Another of Richardson's correspondents, with whom
his acquaintance seems to have begun not long before
the publication of *Clarissa*, was Miss Sarah Westcomb
of Enfield. Richardson had visited this young lady
and her mother in their country-seat, and on his return
wrote enthusiastically of the gardens, the summer-
house, and the " truly serpentine river." Mrs. Westcomb, who was a martyr to gout, and of whom we
hear chiefly as being carried about her grounds in a
sedan-chair all day long, was a widow, and Richardson

seems to have been at once invested with an honorary paternity which permitted him to correspond with Miss Sally at his ease. One of his letters to her from Tunbridge Wells was quoted in the previous chapter, and there is none more interesting in the rest of the batch. The young lady dwells edifyingly on her contempt for " Ranelagh's lofty dome, or Vauxhall's rural scenes," and displays a praiseworthy disdain for the proceedings of the husband-hunting Miss Gunnings, who have been " starring " at Enfield. " May toupees,[1] powder, lace, and essence (the composition of the modern pretty fellows) follow them in troops, to stare, and be stared at, till the more bashful youths give the first blush ! " So writes this gentle moralist; and " her best and good papa " is enraptured at the sentiments. " When women turn seekers," he replies oracularly, " it will not do. Gudgeons may bite; but not even then but by accident, and through inexperience of the wiles of anglers. . . . I hear they [the Gunnings] have been rudely treated at Windsor, as they were at Edmonton." Nevertheless, when Miss Westcomb went shortly afterwards to Ankerwyke (where she fished and caught " no, not even a gudgeon "), she unfortunately enjoyed herself so thoroughly that she forgot to write to her self-constituted parent at North End, who forthwith despatches a seven-page remonstrance to the errant " offspring of his mind." In 1754 Miss Westcomb lost her mother, and not long afterwards, in July 1756, she is happily engaged to a very agreeable young gentleman, Mr. Scudamore, of Kentchurch, Herefordshire. Richardson gave her away in August of that year at St. George's, Hanover Square,

[1] See note, *ante*, p. 81.

and the last we hear of her, in Mrs. Barbauld, is that
she is making use (through *Pamela*) of Mr. Locke's
maxims in the education of her little boy.

One of the groups of correspondents from whom one
would naturally have expected a good deal of interest,
is disappointingly unfruitful; and that is the group
who cluster round Dr. Patrick Delany at Dublin.
Delany had known Richardson as far back as 1739; and
after his second marriage to Mrs. Pendarves, both that
lady, her sister Mrs. Dewes, and her friends Mrs.
Donnellan and Miss Sutton, as well as the Doctor himself, wrote at intervals to Richardson between 1750
and 1758. The theme, as usual, is very much the
"divine Clarissa," and Richardson's other performances,
past and future. Upon the whole, Mrs. Donnellan,
whom one of Mrs. Barbauld's informants remembered
at North End, "a venerable old lady, with sharp-
piercing eyes," is the most interesting. She was unmarried, well-educated, and well-connected; and her
knowledge of polite society was not without its use to
Richardson, always seeking to recruit and supplement
his imagination by actual "documents." Her worst
fault is her playing up to Richardson's petty jealousy
of Fielding, who had now given further offence by the
publication of *Amelia*. Writing on the topic of the
"good man," who was to form the subject of Richardson's next work, Mrs. Donnellan says — "Will you
leave us to Capt. Booth and Betty Thoughtless [Mrs.
Haywood's novel with that title] for our examples?
As for poor Amelia, she is so great a fool we pity her,
but cannot be humble enough to desire to imitate her.
. . . Poor Fielding, I believe, designed to be good,
but did not know how, and in the attempt lost his

genius, low humour." Richardson's reply is a screed
of malevolence. " Will I leave you to Captain Booth ?
Capt. Booth, Madam, has done his own business.
Mr. Fielding has over-written himself, or rather *under*-
written; and in his own journal seems ashamed of his
last piece; and has promised that the same muse shall
write no more for him. The piece, in short, is as
dead, as if it had been published forty years ago, as
to sale." And then he goes on to say that he has
read but the first volume, that he had intended to
go through with it, but that he found the characters
and situations so " wretchedly low and dirty " that he
could not be interested in any one of them, and he
finally winds up with a paragraph of scandalous gossip
touching Fielding, his first wife, his characters, and his
works.

That *Amelia* was not as great a success as *Tom Jones,*
is true; and we have the word of Miss Elizabeth Carter
that the Beaux and Fine Ladies disliked the author's
new type of wifehood, and were unanimous in pronouncing her history to be " very sad stuff " — a verdict
with which Miss Carter — to her credit be it spoken —
does not seem to have concurred. But it is instructive to compare Richardson's shrewish and ill-natured
utterances with the actual passages from the *Covent-
Garden Journal,* to which he makes reference. Fielding brings his book before his own " Court of Censorial
Enquiry." He lets Amelia's accusers speak; but he
disdains to plead her cause against them. " If you,
Mr. Censor, are yourself a Parent, you will view me
with Compassion when I declare I am the Father of
this poor Girl the Prisoner at the Bar; nay, when I
go farther, and avow, that of all my Offspring she is

my favourite Child." He explains what models he
has followed, and then continues, " I do not think my
Child is entirely free from Faults. I know nothing
human that is so; but surely she does not deserve the
Rancour with which she hath been treated by the
Public. However, it is not my Intention, at present,
to make any Defence; but shall submit to a Compromise, which hath been always allowed in this
Court in all Prosecutions for Dulness. I do, therefore,
solemnly declare to you, Mr. Censor, that I will
trouble the World no more with any Children of Mine
by the same Muse." One must be a rival, and a jealous
one, not to feel the effect of these sad and dignified
utterances. But Richardson's spleen was " *nulla medi-
cabilis herba*," and the day after he had written to
Mrs. Donnellan, he breaks out to another correspondent. " It is beyond my conception," he says, " that a
man of family, and who had some learning, and who
really is a writer, should descend so excessively low,
in all his pieces. Who can care for any of his people?
A person of honour asked me, the other day, what he
[Fielding] could mean, by saying, in his *Covent Garden
Journal*, that he had followed Homer and Virgil, in his
Amelia. I answered, that he was justified in saying
so, because he must mean Cotton's *Virgil Travestied ;*
where the women are drabs, and the men scoundrels."
This is sheer insolence; but in regard to the charge of
" lowness " — that bugbear of the earlier students of
humanity in the rough — no answer is required save the
one which Goldsmith made, a few years later, to a
speech by my Lady Blarney. " There's nothing comes
out but the most lowest stuff in nature " — says that
patrician critic. " Not a bit of high life among

them." And Mr. Burchell, very properly, ejaculates — " *Fudge !* " Nevertheless, it was some time before this damaging form of censure ceased to be used and listened to. Fielding referred to it more than once in *Tom Jones,*[1] and Goldsmith, whose bailiff scene in *The Good Natur'd Man* was voted to be " uncommonly low," does the same in *She Stoops to Conquer.* Not until Sentimental Comedy lay dead or dying, in 1780, was Colman able to write, as he did in the Prologue to Miss Lee's *Chapter of Accidents :* —

> " When Fielding, Humour's fav'rite child, appear'd,
>   *Low* was the word — a word each author fear'd,
>   Till chac'd at length, by pleasantry's bright ray,
>   Nature and mirth resumed their legal sway ;
>   And Goldsmith's genius bask'd in open day."

To return to the Delany correspondence. One of Mrs. Delany's youthful friends had been a Miss Kirkham, the daughter of a clergyman. She married the Rev. John Chapone. One of her daughters, Sally Chapone, was practically adopted by the Delanys; and in 1750, when the eldest son, also John Chapone, came to London to study law, Mrs. Dewes, Mrs. Delany's sister, gave him a letter of introduction to Richardson, with whose North End circle he promptly became a favourite. This led to a voluminous correspondence between his mother and Richardson (it occupies more than one of the huge volumes at South Kensington, and is not reprinted by Mrs. Barbauld), largely engrossed by a discussion of the status of women. The letters are not very fruitful in Richardsoniana. Mrs. Chapone, moreover, clever as she was, was not *the* Mrs. Chapone, famous many years after

1 Vols. iii. 6; iv. 94; and Bk. xii. Ch. v.

for her *Letters on the Improvement of the Mind.* That enviable distinction belongs to a young lady who married the John Chapone above referred to, and whose name was Hester, or, more familiarly, Hecky Mulso. She was the daughter of one Thomas Mulso of Twywell, a gentleman of Northamptonshire (also the home of Harriet Byron [1]), and must have been unusually precocious as a child, since, at the tender age of nine, she composed a brief romance entitled *The Loves of Amoret and Melissa.* Her mother, whose chief gift was beauty, discouraged these premature essays. But, dying not many years after, she left Hester mistress of herself, and of her father's house. She contrived to learn French, Italian, and a little Latin; obtained some knowledge of drawing, and won, by her beautiful voice, the name of " linnet," conferred on her by Thomas Edwards. Spending her winters in London, she became acquainted with Richardson, who took a great fancy to a correspondent, who, to use Walpole's word, was as " corresponding " as himself. " He [Richardson] loved " says Mrs. Barbauld, " to draw out her reasoning powers, then beginning to unfold themselves. He engaged her in a controversy on the measure of filial obedience; but her part of it, with the rest of the letters, was withdrawn from the collection after Richardson's death." [2]   It was a subject

---

[1] It is possible that she served Richardson in some respects as a model. According to Mrs. Delany, Mrs. Donnellan thought her " only second-rate as to *politeness of manner,*" and hinted that Richardson's shortcomings in high life might be owing to his faulty pattern.

[2] Three letters from Miss Mulso to Richardson on this theme are included in vol. ii. of her (Mrs. Chapone's) *Works,* 1807. One runs to 49 pages, the other to 55.

upon which he must have also had other correspondents, for there is an epistle (from which we have
already borrowed a quotation) of more than five
closely printed columns upon this theme in *Notes and
Queries* for 24th April 1869, in which, with excursuses
on *Clarissa*, and side strokes at *Tom Jones*, the discussion should surely have been exhausted. The lady
there addressed, however, is not Miss Mulso, but an
unrevealed " Miss G——." Richardson's own epistles
to Miss Mulso, of which Mrs. Barbauld prints several
between 1750 and 1757, are not very engrossing; and
they are largely occupied by the details of the forthcoming *Grandison*. She does not appear to have
followed up her childish romance by anything except
occasional Odes to Mr. Edwards and Miss Carter, one
of which is preserved in that lady's translation of
Epictetus, three papers in the third volume of the
Adventurer ("The Story of Fidelia") and correspondence. Johnson printed some of her notelets in
No. 10 of the *Rambler*. She must have met him
frequently in her visits to North End, and indeed,
in one of her letters to Miss Carter, a year or two
later, gives an account of his bringing blind Miss
Williams with him to tea. " I was charmed," she
says, " with Mr. Johnson's behaviour to Mrs. Williams,
which was like that of a fond father to his daughter."
Miss Mulso is one of the Richardson group concerning
whom one willingly asks for more. She was not one
of Richardson's neck-or-nothing flatterers. He even
described her, playfully of course, as a "little spitfire."
She has the courage of her opinions: she sees the
faults of Johnson and Young, and says so; and she
has a frank and genuine distaste for Fielding (she

liked Amelia, but could not away with Captain Booth),
to which, as it is frank and genuine, we cannot reason-
ably object. Her attachment to John Chapone, which
began almost as soon as she met him, was not followed
by marriage for many years; and when at last, in
December 1760, they were united, he only lived for a
short time, surviving Richardson himself, who was
much attached to him, for little more than two months.
After this, she passes out of the scope of this memoir,
although she lived to become the author of the once
famous *Letters on the Improvement of the Mind*, the
commended of Queen Charlotte, and the "admirable
Mrs. Chapone" of the more serious Bas Bleus. Apparently she did not inherit her mother's personal
attractions, or else lost them in advanced age. "She
concealed very superior attainments and extensive
knowledge" — says the uncompromising Wraxall —
"under one of the most repulsive exteriors that any
woman ever possessed." Gallantry might be disposed
to regard this simply as the verdict of an unsym-
pathetic male. But it is amply confirmed, as regards
the lack of beauty, by Fanny Burney's sister Charlotte,
who met Mrs. Chapone in 1782 at the house of that
lady's relative, the genial and musical Dean of
Winchester, Dr. Newton Ogle. "She looked less
forbidding than usual," says this plain-spoken young
lady; "but she is deadly ugly, to be sure—such African
nose and lips, and such a clunch figure!" ("Clunch" is
a Burney word, meaning "thick-set," or "stumpy.")
Fanny Burney herself is much kinder. "Mrs. Chapone . . . is the most superiorly unaffected creature
you can conceive, and full of *agrémens* from good sense,
talents, and conversational powers, in defiance of age,

infirmities, and uncommon ugliness. I really love as well as admire and esteem her."

North End, besides being a nursery of sentiment, must also have been a hotbed of the affections, for when Miss Mulso was married to John Chapone, her brother Edward Mulso was simultaneously united to the "amiable Pressy," otherwise Miss Prescott, another frequenter of the Richardsonian circle. Mr. Thomas Mulso, the elder, "unwilling to protract [? postpone] the union of two of his children, so long and so unalterably attached as his daughter to Mr. Chapone, and his eldest son to Miss Prescott, arranged his affairs so as to admit of their both being married on the same day." Nor was this the only affair of the kind which seems to have gone on under Richardson's fostering eye. At South Kensington there are traces of the poetical philanderings of a Corydon and Stella whose loves are not running smoothly, despite the ministrations of a "sage Palemon" whose connection with a "grotto" and a "moral page" makes it impossible not to identify him with the author of *Clarissa*.

> "To good Palemon's Grotto fly ;
> For all distress'd, Asylum kind,
>> Where every Sickness of the Mind
>> Sage Palemon knows [how] to heal,
> And soothing Counsel to reveal,
> Advice in Fancy's Garb arrays,
> Instruction with Delight conveys ;
> Mends every Heart that hears his moral Page,
> Adapted well to every State and Age."

The Stella of this very pedestrian idyl — the poem itself is, of course, an Ode — was Miss Susannah Highmore, daughter of the painter Joseph Highmore,

dwelling at the Sign of the Two Lions in Holborn
Row, Lincoln's Inn Fields. Highmore, to whom we
owe so many likenesses of Richardson, was an artist
whose fame has long been eclipsed by that of his
greater contemporaries, but his reputation is now
rising daily. In 1744 he had painted twelve scenes
from *Pamela*, prints from which were advertised in
April of the following year. These scenes were
probably those decorations of Ranelagh to which
Mrs. Haywood refers in her story of *Jenny and Jemmy
Jessamy*. He had also painted Clarissa " in the
Vandyke taste and dress " favoured by Gray and
Horace Walpole; and he made a study of the Harlowe
family from the beginning of the novel.[1] In Mrs.
Barbauld's fifth volume there is an Ode to him by
Thomas Mulso, prompted by his picture of Richard-
son, no doubt the full-length in the National Portrait
Gallery, which is dated 1750.

> " Well can thy running pencil trace
>   The comely features of his honest face,
>   Well canst thou suffuse his eye,
>   With sense and soft humanity ;
>   Good humour too the dimpled cheek,
>   And pleasing countenance bespeak."

Mr. Highmore, however, does not seem to have regarded his daughter's Corydon with the same favour
as did the " sage Palemon." Yet Mr. John Duncombe,
Junior, was not without distinction. He had a literary
father who had written a couple of tragedies; and he
himself was a Cambridge man, who like the younger
Mulso had contributed his paper to the *World* of

---

[1] This picture, in 1780, belonged to T. W. Payler of Ileden
in Kent.

Edward Moore — that "bow of Ulysses in which it was the fashion for men of rank and genius to try their strength." By 1753 he had become the Reverend, and in the following year published *The Feminead; or, Female Genius*, which, notwithstanding the objection of honest Thomas Edwards to "omne quod exit in *ad*," is not without interest, especially as, among the "learned ladies" who constitute its theme, it celebrates some of the bright, particular stars of the North End constellation. The "good Palemon" naturally comes very early to the front, and without disguise, in this artless performance, which may still be read at large in the fourth volume of Pearch's collection : —

> " Thou, who so oft with pleas'd, but anxious care,
> Hast watch'd the dawning genius of the fair,
> With wonted smiles wilt hear thy friend display
> The various graces of the female lay;
> Studious from Folly's yoke their mind to free,
> And aid the generous cause espous'd by thee."

Then, beginning with the "matchless Orinda" (Mrs. Katherine Phillips), and Anne, Countess of Winchilsea, the writer, not without due reprobation of your Behns and Manleys (and even Pilkingtons), progresses to what probably was the prime object of his unpremeditated effort, praise of Miss Carter, Miss Farrer of the *Ode to Cynthia*, Miss "Delia" Mulso, and Miss "Eugenia" Highmore, — "the muse's pupil from her tend'rest years" : —

> " Improving tasks her peaceful hours beguile,
> The sister arts on all her labours smile,
> And while the Nine their votary inspire,
> 'One dips the pencil and one strings the lyre,' [1]

[1] This is line 70 of Pope's *Epistle to Mr. Jervas*.

O may her life's clear current smoothly glide,
Unruffled by misfortune's boist'rous tide,
So while the charmer leads her blameless days
With that content which she so well displays,
Her own Honoria we in her shall view,
And think her allegoric vision true."

The last reference — a note informs us — is to "an ingenious allegory" by Miss Highmore, in which "two pilgrims, Fidelio and Honoria, after a fruitless search for the palace of Happiness, are at last conducted to the house of Content."

It was not until just before Richardson's death that John Duncombe and Susannah Highmore arrived at that temple of Content over the door of which is written Matrimony. They were married in April 1761, and, in the future into which we need not follow them, lived happily for some three-and-twenty years. Mrs. Barbauld prints some of the letters which passed between Richardson and his young friend (Miss Highmore was of course a supplementary daughter); but with the exception of the invitation to Tunbridge Wells quoted in the last chapter, they are not of absorbing interest. One of them, which refers to the young lady's kindness for Mr. Duncombe, displays a good deal of that teasing raillery in which Richardson seems to have excelled,[1] and incidentally he gives it a better name than he knew when he says that Mr. Edwards accuses him of loving like "Polly" in the *Beggar's Opera* to "tarantalise" — a word which, for compound expressiveness, might have been invented by the author of *Alice in Wonderland*. He confirms what

[1] "My Pen is sometimes a very perverse one, and loves to tease and amuse," — he writes to Lady Bradshaigh in October 1753.

he had once written to Young as to his preference for
writing over reading. "What stores of knowledge do
I lose, by my incapacity of reading, and by my having
used myself to write, till I can do nothing else, nor
hardly that." Elsewhere he says, "I don't wonder you
are in such raptures with Spenser! What an imagination! What an invention! What painting! What
colouring displayed throughout the works of that
admirable author! and yet for want of time, or opportunity, I have not read his *Fairy Queen* through in
series, or at a heat, as I may call it " — which last
words oddly suggest Mr. Silas Wegg on *The Decline
and Fall.* "I haven't been not to say right slap through
him, very lately," — are the words of that wooden-
legged impostor. Richardson was no impostor; but
it may fairly be doubted, whether he too had ever been
in, as Macaulay puts it, "at the death of the Blatant
Beast." In another letter he speaks of entertaining
Mrs. Donnellan ("a woman of fine parts, and great
politeness") with Miss Sutton at breakfast; and later,
in a Pepysian passage, draws a picture of old Cibber
reciting his own translations from Horace on a hot day,
"till he was in a breathing, and wiped and acted like
anything, and everybody was pleased." A further
passage (from a letter to Mr. Duncombe) shows that
he is meditating a change of residence; and what is
more, that he has already selected a new house. "On
Parson's Green, between Chelsea and Fulham (pro-
pitious be the name of the place!), on the side of the
King's Road to Fulham, Putney, Richmond, etc., have
I pitched, at last, my tent. There is a porch at the
door (an old monastery-like house) in which my friends,
such even as will not come on purpose, will find it

difficult, as they pass by, to avoid seeing the old man, who, if he lives, proposes often in it to reconnoitre the Green, and watch for them." This letter is dated 24th August 1754. But, as we shall see, it was not until the end of October, that he actually took up residence in his new home.

Of the remaining letter-writers for this period, with one exception, none is of great importance. Mrs. Barbauld prints a number of epistles to and from an Irish clergyman named Skelton, who helped Richardson to get in his Irish debts; but they have little biographical interest. Of the rest, a letter to a Mr. Defreval of Paris [1] in January 1751, when the extended edition of *Clarissa* was at press, contains some personal traits. Richardson complains of the correspondence which the book has brought upon him, — of his nervous infirmities that "time mends not." "*Clarissa*," he says, "has almost killed me. You know how my business engages me. You know by what snatches of time I write, that I may not neglect that, and that I may preserve that independency which is the comfort of my life. I never sought out of myself for patrons. My own industry, and God's providence, have been my whole reliance." In the Postscript comes a thrust at *Tom Jones*. "*Tom Jones* is a dissolute book. Its run is over, even with us. Is it true, that France has virtue enough to refuse a licence for such a profligate performance?" This story has the support of Scott,[2]

---

[1] Mr. J. B. Defreval was the author of the first commendatory letter in the first edition of *Pamela*, which bears the initials "J. B. D. F."

[2] In all probability Scott's authority was Watson's *Life of Fielding*, 1807, p. 107, where it is stated that "the Council of State of France . . . issued an arrêt, suppressing the publica-

who says that " French delicacy, which, on so many
occasions, has strained at a gnat, and swallowed a
camel, by an *arrêt* prohibited the circulation of a
bungling abridgement of De la Place, entitled a translation." But Mr. Defreval, in his reply to Richardson,
does not believe it.   " I am sorry to say it, but you do
my countrymen more honour than they truly deserve,
in surmising that they had virtue enough to refuse a
licence to *Tom Jones:* I think it a profligate performance upon your pronouncing it such [!], for I have
never read the piece, though much extolled ; but it has
had a vast run here this good while, and considering
how things go on, I don't believe there is now a book
dissolute enough to be refused admittance among us,
since pieces of the worst tendency are sure of getting
it by hook or by crook."

Reference was made above to one among Richardson's
correspondents whose letters were of rather more
importance than those just mentioned. This was the
unknown admirer, who in her communications adopted
the name of " Mrs. Belfour." She continued to write
to Richardson even after her disappointment in regard
to the ending of *Clarissa;* and he naturally began to
be somewhat curious about the position and personal
appearance of a lady who was evidently a reader after
his own heart, and as a writer so indefatigable that
she did not know when to leave off. She announced
that when she came to town she would see him
unknown to himself ; and he replied by endeavouring

tion and sale of it " [*i.e.* De la Place's version].   Or it may have
been the following : — " ∴ The newspapers inform us, that the
celebrated history of *Tom Jones* has been suppressed in *France*
as an immoral work " (*Monthly Review*, 1750, ii. p. 432).

to induce her to visit North End.   A good deal of
finessing ensued on both sides : — on his, to identify
the lady at certain places where she announced that
she would be; on hers, to see him without being seen.
In order that she might make no possible mistake in
this preliminary investigation, he gave her a detailed
description of himself which has long been recognised
as a faithful picture.   " I go thro' the Park once or
twice a week to my little retirement; but I will for
a week together be in it every day three or four
hours, at your command, till you tell me you have
seen a person who answers to this description, namely,
Short, rather plump than emaciated, notwithstanding
his complaints : about five foot five inches : fair wig;
lightish cloth coat, all black besides : one hand generally in his bosom, the other a cane in it, which he
leans upon under the skirts of his coat usually, that it
may imperceptibly serve as a support, when attacked
by sudden tremors or startings, and dizziness . . . looking directly foreright, as passers-by would imagine ;
but observing all that stirs on either hand of him
without moving his short neck ; hardly ever turning
back : of a light-brown complexion; teeth not yet
failing him ; smoothish faced and ruddy cheeked : at
sometimes looking to be about sixty-five, at other
times much younger : a regular even pace, stealing
away ground, rather than seeming to rid it: a gray
eye, too often overclouded by mistinesses from the
head : by chance lively ; very lively it will be, if he
have hope of seeing a lady whom he loves and
honours : his eye always on the ladies; if they have
very large hoops, he looks down and supercilious, and
as if he would be thought wise, but perhaps the sillier

for that: as he approaches a lady, his eye is never
fixed first upon her face, but upon her feet, and thence
he raises it up, pretty quickly for a dull eye; and one
would think (if we thought him at all worthy of
observation) that from her air and (the last beheld)
her face, he sets her down in his mind as *so* or *so*, and
then passes on to the next object he meets; only then
looking back, if he greatly likes or dislikes, as if he
would see if the lady appear to be all of a piece, in
the one light or in the other."

In Mrs. Belfour's reply to this, which is dated 16th
December 1749, she is still deliberating. She cannot
accept the invitation to North End. But she has sent
his description to a friend. The description of the
friend, however, is evidently a description of herself.
" She is middle-aged, middle-sized, a degree above
plump, brown as an oak wainscot, a good deal of
country red in her cheeks; altogether a plain woman,
but nothing remarkably forbidding." " She will attend
the Park every fine warm day, between the hours of
one and two." Between the hours of one and two
accordingly we must imagine Richardson offering himself for inspection. But " Mrs. Belfour," too, possesses
the gift of "tarantalising." By some accident, or
whim of the sender, he did not receive her letter of
the 16th December until Saturday, the 30th. On the
following Sunday, having been prevented by what
almost seems an opportune indisposition from going
to North End, he went into the Park with nothing
but a sea-biscuit in his pocket, in hopes of seeing his
Incognita. On the Saturday following (the 6th Jan.)
he " walked backwards and forwards in the Mall till
past her friend's time of being there," and was mani-

festly a little put out.   Nevertheless he continues to
perambulate the Mall and Constitution Hill, wearying
his daughter Patty, and her friend Miss Collier, by the
assiduity of his search.   At last, on February the 17th,
she passes him four times without revealing herself.
" I knew you," she writes a week later, " by your own
description, at least three hundred yards off, walking
in the Park between the trees and the Mall. . . . You
looked at me every time we passed; but I put on
so unconcerned a countenance, that I am almost sure
I deceived you."   It was March, nevertheless, before
they met.   But before that time, and indeed before
the occurrence just referred to, Richardson had discovered his correspondent's real name.   She had
visited Highmore's studio to see the Clarissa pictures, and Highmore's inquisitive French servant
had managed to ascertain who she was.

She proved to be the wife of Sir Roger Bradshaigh
of Haigh, near Wigan, in Lancashire, a gentleman of
much landed property in the coal country, but not
rich.   She was childless, devoted to her husband ; and,
says Mrs. Barbauld, " bore the character of a most
worthy, pious and charitable woman," but rather
hearty and active than " polished."   Indeed, though
she was fairly well read and intelligent, she seems to
have been needlessly unwilling to incur the reproach
of exceptional learning.   Especially was she anxious
not to be regarded as the correspondent of a live
author.   She begs Richardson on no account to make
her name public, and to engage Mr. Highmore, or
whoever may be in the secret, to use a like discretion.
" Though I glory in it myself, and have with pride
confessed it to some select friends, yet, I know, by

the ill-judging and the envious, I should be thought conceited, and too self-sufficient, in corresponding with one so far my superior in understanding, and an author." She carried this to such an extent that when later Richardson sent her his portrait — a portrait which is said still to be preserved by the family — she altered the name above the frame from Richardson to *Dicken*son, that the questions asked her about her distant friend might not cause embarrassment or betray her unwittingly.

In Mrs. Barbauld's collection, Lady Bradshaigh's correspondence under her own name and that of "Mrs. Belfour" occupies rather more than a volume and a half, and even this does not include many of the letters at South Kensington. "They," says Mrs. Barbauld rather grimly, "together with Richardson's answers, would alone make several volumes, I believe as many as the whole of this publication [*i.e.* six], a proof, by the way, that the bookseller and the editor have had some mercy on the public." It would be idle, in the narrower space available here, to attempt to give any adequate account of this very extensive material. Some quotations have already been made in connection with *Clarissa;* others will naturally be made in speaking of *Sir Charles Grandison*. And it must be confessed that the matter on either side is scarcely enthralling. When the progress of either *Clarissa* or its successor is not under consideration, the interest flags appreciably. Here and there, however, are to be found items of literary intelligence. In one case Lady Bradshaigh refers to a letter on the change in the manners of women, which Richardson had addressed to the *Rambler* (No. 97, for 19th February 1751), in order to tell him that, as it was so much better written than the other papers, a friend had supposed it from the pen of some one concerned in the *Spectators.* Johnson, who had praised the writer in his introductory words by the memorable commendation that he had "enlarged the knowledge of human nature, and taught the passions to move at the command of virtue," would probably not have endorsed this opinion as to style. It seems, however, to be a fact that none of Johnson's own efforts had so large a sale as Richardson's contribution. Another thing discussed is Lord Orrery's *Remarks on Swift*, to which Richardson, having met His Lordship in Millar's shop and exchanged civilities, is naturally well disposed. It was Orrery who first started the story of Swift's marriage to Stella; and it is interesting to notice that Richardson professes to have heard of the marriage as "a certain truth" long before Orrery had written. And he adds that his informant was a lady of goodness, no enemy but to what was bad in Swift, — a description which may perhaps stand for Mrs. Delany.[1] In a later letter of 24th February 1753, there is an unusual amount of bookish chit-chat. The rival Ciceros of Cibber and Conyers Middleton are compared; and there is mention of *The Female Quixote*, whose authoress, Charlotte Lenox, was often a visitor at North End, and had complimented *Clarissa* in type, a kindness which the "admirable Writer" thereof affects to deprecate. Another reference is to Moore's

[1] Her husband believed in it. "Your account of his [Swift's] marriage," he says to Orrery, "is, I am satisfied, true" (*Observations upon Lord Orrery's Remarks on the Life and Writings of Dr. Jonathan Swift*, 1754, p. 53).

Gamester, which Richardson had heard Garrick read; and there is an expression of heartfelt regret that Young's tragedy of *The Brothers* should be hopelessly overshadowed by the *Earl of Essex*, another tragedy by Lord Chesterfield's bricklayer poet, Henry Jones. But the most interesting passage of this letter refers to the foreign versions of the writer's works. " My vanity . . . has been raised by a present sent me of a translation of *Clarissa*, in the German language, in eight volumes, from the celebrated Dr. Haller, Vice-Chancellor of the University of Göttingen; and by two volumes neatly printed, of the same, in Dutch, by an eminent hand, M. Stinstra, of Haarlingen, in Friesland, who is going on with the translation, two volumes at a time; also by a present of the same work in twelve thin volumes in French, translated by the Abbé Prévost, author of the *Dean of Colerain*, and other pieces. But this gentleman has thought fit to omit some of the most affecting parts; as the death of Belton; Miss Howe's lamentation over the corpse of her friend; Sinclair's death and remorse; and many of the letters (though with some commendations) that passed between Lovelace and Belford, after Clarissa's death, with some apologies, that, a lady, who understands the language says, imply a reflexion on his nation.[1] He treats the story as a true one; and says, in one place, that the English editor has often sacrificed his story to moral instructions, warnings, etc. — the very motive with me, of the story's being

---

[1] " Who understands the language " — is proof that Richardson read no French. Prévost, it may be added, did not, as we shall see (*post* p. 201 *n.*), omit the " reflexion on his nation " contained in the prefatory letters to *Pamela*.

written at all." This almost reads as if this was
Richardson's first communication with Prévost. But
the Preface to the French version of *Pamela* says
distinctly that that version had made "avec la
participation de l'auteur, qui a eu la bonté de nous
fournir un petit nombre d'additions et de corrections"
— as well as some "portraits" of the characters.

Lady Bradshaigh, besides being the most assiduous,
is also the last of Richardson's correspondents. Indeed her final letter is dated after his death, and is
addressed to one of his married daughters, Mrs.
Bridgen. She herself survived until 1789, when she
died at the age of eighty. But there must have been
many visitors to the hospitable house at North End
who do not figure among the writers of letters, or
only figure rarely. The already-mentioned Mrs.
Charlotte Lenox, for instance, was often there, and
could scarcely recall an occasion upon which "her
host had not rehearsed at least one, but probably two
or three voluminous letters, if he found her in the
humour of listening with attention." Miss Carter
(whose *Ode on Wisdom* Richardson had boldly annexed
while in manuscript for the second volume of *Clarissa*)
and her friend, Miss Talbot, again, were, no doubt,
frequently breakfast guests, like Miss Sutton and
Mrs. Donnellan. The men visitors were fewer. But
Cibber, as we have seen, came occasionally, and doubtless Speaker Onslow, as well as Thomas Edwards
and Dr. Young. Johnson, we know, visited at both
houses, and Hogarth. Indeed, it was under Richardson's roof that the Painter first saw the Lexicographer.
In 1753, immediately after the execution of Dr.
Archibald Cameron, for complicity in the '45, Hogarth

and Richardson were discussing that event. There was another person standing at a window in the room, shaking his head, and rolling himself about in a ridiculous manner. Hogarth took him for some one of defective intelligence, placed under his friend's care. But presently the figure lumbered forward, and burst into an animated invective against George the Second, whose clemency had been in question, displaying such an unexpected power of oratory that the painter thought him inspired. He often heard the great man afterwards, but at this meeting, it is expressly stated, they were not made known to one another.

CHAPTER VI

In the first chapter of this book, mention was made of a certain grotto or summer-house in the garden at North End, where Richardson was in the habit of reading his productions to a select circle of admirers. Miss Susannah Highmore, who inherited something of her father's talent, has left a little picture of one of these sessions. Whether the fair artist, after the fashion of the draughtsmen of her day, has yielded overmuch to the seductions of perspective, we know not; but what she depicts is a rather spacious chamber entered from without by two descending steps, so that its floor would appear to be slightly below the level of the ground. It is scantly furnished, but extensive enough to accommodate a party of seven, that is, in addition to the author, three ladies and three gentlemen. Richardson, "in his usual morning dress," a velvet cap, and the night- or dressing-gown of the period, sits to the left with crossed legs (as in Chamberlin's portrait), intent upon the latest instalment of the manuscript of Grandison. To his left is Mr. Mulso, senior; and further still to the left, on a seat by the door, his son, Mr. Edward Mulso. At the opposite side of the apartment, grouped round a table, are the remainder of the company. Miss

138

Mulso, a dignified young woman, whose figure here, at all events, does not deserve the depreciatory epithet which Charlotte Burney bestowed upon it, comes first. Next to Miss Mulso is Miss Prescott, who, as we know, subsequently became Mrs. Edward Mulso; and next to Miss Prescott, the Rev. John Duncombe, who is taking a pinch of snuff with a gesture which would do credit to Chesterfield himself. By him sits the damsel of his choice, the artist, Miss Highmore. The ladies wear sacques, hoops (for the nonce disposed over their seats), and Pamela hats; the gentlemen, in the ordinary costume of the day, are elegantly posed in attitudes of attention.

The little picture bears no date. But it must have been executed not long before July 1751, as it is mentioned in a letter addressed at that time by Miss Mulso to Miss Highmore, referring to " the dear circle at North End, which your pencil so prettily described. You do not know," says the future Mrs. Chapone, to whom we must assume that the drawing once belonged, " how much pleasure I take in surveying that sketch, nor how often I contemplate every figure in it, and recall the delights of that day."[1] From these last words it would appear that this particular reading was a somewhat exceptional one. But, according to Mrs. Barbauld, it was Richardson's practice to write in the grotto before the family were up, communicating afterwards to the party at breakfast the daily advance of his

[1] Miss Mulso, as already stated, was herself an amateur artist. " I had great pleasure in seeing in Mr. Richardson's hands an exceeding like picture of you, drawn by Miss Mulso this last summer — Do not be scandalised ; he cannot possibly wear it in his snuff-box " (*Miss Talbot to Mrs. Carter*, 12th August 1756).

labours. "Then," says Mrs. Barbauld, in an oft-
quoted passage, "began the criticisms, the pleadings,
for Harriet Byron or Clementina; every turn and
every incident was eagerly canvassed, and the author
enjoyed the benefit of knowing beforehand how his
situations would strike." It was here also that he
studied his guests, of whom he always had a working
assortment on hand, whose own little partialities and
entanglements were frequently developed under his
eye, "becoming the subject of grave advice or lively
raillery." "I have often sat by in company," he tells
a correspondent, "and been silently pleased with the
opportunity given me, by different arguers, of looking
into the hearts of some of them, through windows that
at other times have been closed." It is clear that he
was always using his "flower-garden of ladies" either
as critics of his work, or as object-lessons in sensibility.
"You cannot imagine, Madam," he says, in another
letter to a different person, "how much the Characters
of Clarissa, of Miss Howe, of Lovelace, of Mr. Hickman, have let me into the Hearts and Souls of my
Acquaintance of both Sexes, some of which, those of
Sophia and Tom Jones, have greatly confirmed."

Clarissa had been published in 1747–48, and *Tom
Jones* in 1749. Whether *Sir Charles Grandison* would
have been written at all if *Tom Jones* had never existed,
is a speculation upon which it would now be fruitless
to enter, although it is probable that there is more
connection between the two than is generally imagined.
Tom Jones, at all events, was a hero with many of the
other sex; and it is equally certain that he was not
at all a hero after Richardson's pattern. It is quite
in the nature of things that Richardson should think

himself capable of producing a better model. Moreover, he had gained strength enormously. When he
wrote *Pamela*, his native genius for minute analysis
was possibly as strong as it was when he wrote *Clarissa ;*
but his full knowledge of his own gifts was still to
come, his powers were untrained, and his experience
was narrow and limited. His books had now made
him many friends ; and he had around him a circle of
admirers, who were far more capable of stimulating
his invention, and directing his efforts, than the
"worthy-hearted wife" and her young lady friend,
who, in his little writing-closet at Salisbury Court,
had listened daily to the story of the distresses of
Pamela Andrews. And it was the peculiarity of his
diffident, half-educated nature, that he required the
constant encouragement of a somewhat exaggerated
applause. In the strong wind of a robust criticism his
inventive faculties would have been shrivelled, and his
imagination dried up; but in the warm-winged adula-
tion of the little consistory he gathered about him, he
expanded, bloomed, and flourished. Their suggestions
served to recruit and fructify his easily-fatigued fancy,
and although his advisers probably imagined that
they were helping him a good deal more than he
would have allowed, there can be no doubt that they
did afford material aid. With the plot of another
Clarissa they were incapable of supplying him ; but
when he sat down to write *Sir Charles Grandison*, he
was far better equipped for a fresh undertaking than
he had ever been before.

We begin to hear of *Sir Charles Grandison* at the
close of 1749, when Lady Bradshaigh, still masquer-
ading as "Mrs. Belfour," urges Richardson to give

the world his idea of a good man and fine gentleman combined. In his reply, he demurs and hesitates. He has doubts as to drawing such a character, looking to the favour shown to Lovelace, and the ill-reception accorded to the excellent but unattractive Hickman of his earlier book. The question comes again to the front in June of the following year. He has been visited at North End by Mrs. Donnellan and Miss Sutton, " both very intimate with one Clarissa Harlowe : and both extremely earnest with him to give them a *good man.*" The good man, it is understood, is to be wonderfully polite, but no Hickman. " How can we hope that ladies will not think a good man a tame man ? " he asks Miss Highmore. When Mrs. Donnellan gets back to Epsom, in acknowledging the *Meditations,* and other books which Richardson has sent to her, she returns to the subject. " I fancy," she says, " if you would draw a fine man, as you have a woman, the young ladies would become your correspondents more readily." From the reply, the idea is evidently taking shape in Richardson's mind. Will not the ladies tell him what they want ? What *is* the ideal man to do, and what is he *not* to do ? — in order to acquire and maintain an exemplary character. It would be merely futile to avoid leading him into difficulties, such as challenges, etc. (to which as a good man he would be particularly exposed), simply because he could not, consistently with his character, be honourably extricated from such a position. Then ought he not to have great distresses, and be made happy at last, at least as far as this life is concerned ? The young ladies must help him to make his hero. " It is more in the power of young ladies than they seem to

imagine, to make a fine man." Nevertheless he fears
— very much fears — that the fine man when made,
would not have the suffrages of the sex unless he had
more of Lovelace than of Hickman in his composition.

In his next letter, to Mrs. Delany's sister, Mrs.
Dewes, he seems to imply that he had already
attempted a beginning since he refers to the subject —
" two or three letters of which you saw." But he continues to be doubtful. His business is engrossing;
his time of life too advanced ; the task proposed, above
all, exceptionally arduous. How shall he draw — he
asks once more — a man that *good* men would approve,
and that the young ladies of the age would think
amiable ? Mrs. Donnellan endeavours to get over or
round the duelling difficulty by suggesting that the
hero's fighting should have been done before the
reader makes his acquaintance, so that, his courage
having been proved beyond question, he should be
immune from insult. Some faults he must have, she
admits — some failings from passion, "but must be
soon recovered by reason and religion." "In short,"
she adds, "he must have more of Miss Howe than of
Clarissa" — a sentiment which almost justifies the
pleasant jibe that Sir Charles Grandison is one of
the author's chief feminine characters. And so the
discussion goes on, without advancing greatly. Nothing, admits Mrs. Delany, is "more difficult than to
make him brave, and avoid duelling, that reigning
curse." "But how to ward off a challenge, and preserve his character, is a task only to be undertaken
by the author of *Clarissa*."

Then there are other obstacles, — for example, the
delineation of fashionable society. How can that be

compassed ?   " How should I," writes Richardson to
Mrs. Dewes, " a very ordinary man, unlearned, all my
early years employed to get a mechanic business for a
livelihood [a business which, he writes elsewhere, still
sometimes employs him eighteen hours out of the
twenty-four] . . . touch those subjects as they require,
the scenes, most of them, in high life." Mrs. Donnellan,
to whom he appeals, is not very practically helpful.
" You are very humble in desiring help and scenes to
be given you.   Indeed the manners of high and
fashionable life consist in a sort of routine, as the
French call it, which varies so often, that it must be
catched flying." [1]   " The present turn," she adds, " is
taste "; and she goes on to quote Mrs. Montagu on
Foote's new farce with that title, then [1752] acting
at Drury Lane.   " Taste," she considers, " would be a
very proper subject for Sir Charles Grandison to
expatiate on."   In a letter to Lady Bradshaigh
another difficulty is revealed.   " I own that a good
woman is my favourite character, and that I can do
twenty agreeable things for her, none of which would
appear in a striking light in a man."   Yet, in spite of
all these drawbacks, the book seems to be insensibly
making way.   Before the end of 1751 he had sent a
sketch to Mrs. Donnellan ; and by the middle of the
following year, it has advanced considerably.   " The
good man " . . . he writes, " is grown under my hands

---

[1] Mrs. Donnellan is here, of course, referring, not to that
sort of good breeding which, as Scott says, is "natural and
unchangeable," but to that other, which, "consisting of an acquaintance with the evanescent manners and fashions of the
day, is merely conventional, and is perpetually changing, like
the modes of dress observed in the same circles" (*Lives of the
Novelists*, 1825, ii. 62).

from a thin gentleman, as I designed him, to a gigantic bulk. And there are so many things that may be done, and said, and written by a common man that cannot by a good man, that delicacies arise on delicacies. " . . . " I have, however, written a great deal, thro' an encrease of my nervous malady, and a business that is enough to engage my whole attention: how well, is another question. But if it be likely to disgrace what I have done, it will never see the light. Hitherto it has not been disapproved of by some people of judgment, who have seen parts of it. And this I can say, I borrow not from anybody, no, not from myself; and I think whatever it wants, it has variety."

After this fashion, between speculations whether his good man should drink, and how much; appeals to Miss Sutton for a "racketing conversation," piping hot from high life; threats to Miss Mulso that he would give the book a "bad ending" (which cause that excitable critic to rave and execrate him), and lamentings over his own hypochondria and the illness of his daughter Anne — the new novel proceeds, and increases apace. At last, in November 1753, between the *Stage Coach* and the *History of Lucy Wellers*, appeared in the *Gentleman's Magazine*, an announcement of the publication in 12° of the first four volumes of the *History of Sir Charles Grandison : in a Series of Letters published from the Originals.* — *By the Editor of Pamela and Clarissa*, London : Printed for S. Richardson, and sold by Dodsley in Pall Mall and others. In December, the month in which Hogarth published his *Analysis of Beauty*, followed two more volumes; and in March 1754, when Garrick had issued his *Ode to Pelham*, and

L

Fielding was lying ill at Bow Street, the book was completed by a seventh and final volume. Concurrently with this *seven* volume duodecimo edition was issued a *six* volume edition in octavo. The whole of the work in this case came out within five months, whereas the publication of *Clarissa* had extended over a year. But the volumes, or part of them, must have been in print before November 1753, as Johnson acknowledged the receipt of some of them, probably the first four, in September.[1] "It is a kind of tyrannical kindness," he says, on the 26th, "to give only so much at a time, as makes more longed for; but that [he added graciously] will probably be thought, even of the whole, when you have given it." He is too honest, however, not to observe upon the Preface, in which Richardson, while in one place practically admitting the authorship of the book, says in another — "How such remarkable collections of private letters fell into the editor's hand he hopes the reader will not think it very necessary to enquire." Johnson's comment upon this is thoroughly characteristic. "If you were to require my opinion which part [in the

---

[1] From a letter to Miss Talbot, dated 21 Sept. 1753, Miss Carter had received them still earlier. "Mr. Richardson has been so good as to send four volumes of his most charming work. . . . Everybody, I am sure, will be struck with the advantageous difference of the language, though but few can observe it with the peculiar pleasure that I do." These last words lead Miss Carter's editor to suggest that Miss Talbot had revised the book. (*Carter's Letters*, 1819 (3rd ed.), ii. 27–9.) But Lady Bradshaigh read part of it in manuscript, and in one of his letters to that lady, Richardson says of the volumes —"Are not their Being owing more to you, than to any other one Person in the World?" Clearly Sir Charles must have had many sponsors.

preface] should be changed, I should be inclined to
the suppression of that part which seems to disclaim
the composition.[1] What is modesty, if it deserts from
truth ? Of what use is the disguise by which nothing
is concealed ? You must forgive this, because it is
meant well." Richardson no doubt took the hint, for
the offending words are not to be found in the existing preface to the novel.

Although there is less plot in *Sir Charles Grandison*
than in *Clarissa*, there is a much larger list of characters, whom the author has oddly grouped as Men,
Women, and Italians, — a plan which recalls Lady
Mary's distribution of humanity into Men, Women,
and Herveys. There is, however, no reason for supposing that in this instance Richardson intended any
subtlety of classification. The story, such as it is, runs
as follows : — Miss Harriet Byron is an orphan of great
personal charms — a little "clunch," perhaps, like
Miss Mulso — who has been educated by her grand-
parents in a most exemplary way. Having, moreover,
a comfortable fortune of fifteen thousand pounds, she
is fully equipped, in eighteenth-century phraseology,
" with all the Accomplishments necessary to render
the Marriage State truly happy," and she is consequently an object of much interested solicitude to
the country gentlemen of the vicinity. At the opening
of the story, she has quitted the house of her uncle,
George Selby, Esq., where she lives, in order to visit
her London cousins, Mr. and Mrs. Reeves, leaving
behind her three disconsolate admirers, Mr. Greville

---

[1] Mrs. Barbauld prints " competition." But " composition,"
which is suggested by Dr. Birkbeck Hill in reproducing this
letter, is obviously intended.

(who describes her at length in a letter to a friend),
Mr. Fenwick, and Mr. Orme.   On reaching town, new
suitors arrive hot-foot, one being a gentleman named
Fowler, who wooes her through his uncle, Sir Rowland
Meredith an importunate old bachelor in a full-buckled
wig and gold-buttoned coat.   To him follows Sir
Hargrave Pollexfen, a bold-eyed, rakehelly baronet,
of a large estate, who is described as voluble, handsome, and genteel, pretty tall, and about twenty-eight
or thirty.   This is one of Richardson's libertines on
the Lovelace pattern.   He falls deeply in love with
the captivating heroine, and does not in the least dis-
semble his passion.   Miss Byron, being pressed to
explain why she cannot receive his addresses, tells
him frankly, and much to his disgust, that she has no
opinion of his morals.   He afterwards renews his suit
in a way of which the following may serve as a
sample : —

"You objected to my morals, madam : Have you
any other objection ?

Need there be any other ?

But I can clear myself.

To God, and to your conscience, then do it, Sir.
I want you not to clear yourself to me.

But, madam, the clearing myself to you would be
clearing myself to God, and my conscience.

What language is this, Sir ?   But you can be
nothing to me : Indeed you can be nothing to me —
Rise, Sir; rise, or I leave you.

I made an effort to go.   He caught my hand,
and arose — Then kissed it, and held it between
both his. . . .

Your objections? I insist upon knowing your objections. My *person*, madam — Forgive me, I am not used to boast — My *person*, madam ——

Pray, Sir Hargrave.

— Is not contemptible. My *fortune* ——

God bless you, Sir, with your fortune.

— Is not inconsiderable. My *morals* ——

Pray, Sir Hargrave ! Why this enumeration to me ?

— Are as unexceptionable as those of most young men of fashion in the present age.

[I am sorry if this be true, thought I to myself.]

You have reason I hope, Sir, to be glad of that.

My *descent* ——

Is honourable, Sir, no doubt.

My *temper* is not bad. I am thought to be a man of vivacity, and of chearfulness — I have *courage*, madam — And this should have been seen, had I found reason to dread a competitor in your favour.

I thought you were enumerating your *good* qualities, Sir Hargrave.

Courage, madam, magnanimity in a man, madam ——

Are great qualities, Sir. Courage in a right cause, I mean. Magnanimity, you know, Sir, is greatness of mind.

And so it is; and I hope ——"

And so the discussion proceeds until it is closed by Miss Byron's positive declaration that she will never more receive Sir Hargrave's visits, an announcement which naturally drives him to desperation, after which the letter placidly concludes with a description of the dress in which the young lady is to flutter the pretty fellows at a masquerade at the Haymarket on the following night. It is one of those enumerations in which Richardson delights, and is supposed to indicate an Arcadian princess. "*Des bergers, — on ne voit que cela partout,*" says the wondering Monsieur Jourdain in Molière's play; but he might well have marvelled at this one, who wore a white Paris net sort of cap, glittering with spangles, and encircled by a chaplet of artificial flowers, with a little white feather perking from the left ear; a Venetian mask; blond lace tucker and ruffles; blue satin waistcoat trimmed with silver Point d'Espagne, and set off with bugles [beads] and spangles; a blue satin petticoat to match, without a hoop ("They wore not hoops in Arcadia"); a scarf of white Persian silk, and a large Indian fan.

The next step, of course, is an abduction. At the masquerade Sir Hargrave, with the assistance of a servant whom he has suborned, contrives to carry off Miss Byron in her chair and masquerade costume to a house at Lisson Green (now Lisson Grove) inhabited by a widow and her two daughters, who, "for a consideration," have no scruples in helping him to an honourable marriage. No ruin is intended—she is expressly assured. One of the richest and noblest men in England is dying for her. She is not engaged, he contends, and therefore must and shall be his, or murder may follow, for he is resolved to be the death of any lover whom she may encourage. And thereupon a Fleet parson is produced, who is depicted by the author with that broad Hogarthian brush which he usually employs for those of his subordinate characters who have no character at all. He was "a vast tall, big-boned, splay-footed man," with "a shabby gown; as shabby a wig; a huge red pimply face; and a nose

that hid half of it, when he looked on one side, and he
seldom looked fore-right." . . . " He had a dog's-ear'd
common-prayer book in his hand, which once had been
gilt; opened . . . at the page of matrimony." To
make matters worse, he snuffled horribly, and when he
parted his pouched mouth, " the tobacco hung about
his great yellow teeth." In the scene that follows, this
" unholy minister " — to use the appropriate language
of the table of " Contents "— " endeavours to commence
the solemn service of the church." But the agitation
of the lady, and her frenzied appeals to the women
folk present, render this impracticable. At last, endeavouring in her terror to escape from the room, she
is seriously hurt, and her tormentor is alarmed. The
parson and his clerk, who have been waiting develop-
ments in the chimney-corner over a jug of ale, hastily
beat a retreat; and the baffled Sir Hargrave has nothing
for it but to muffle his prey in a cloak and capuchin,
and hurry her off in a carriage to his country-house
at Windsor, telling inquirers on the road that he is
taking home a runaway wife, who (like Hogarth's Lady
Squanderfield) has been escaping from a masquerade
to a lover. But the deliverer is at hand. On Houns-
low Heath they are encountered by another chariot
and six, containing a very fine gentleman indeed. He
persists in responding to Miss Byron's appeals for help ;
twists Sir Hargrave out of his coach with such energy
as to make that vehicle rock again ; flings him under
the hind wheel ; neatly snaps his silver-hilted sword
in two, and politely placing the lady in his own
equipage, bears her off triumphantly to the house of
his brother-in-law, the Earl of L., at Colnebrook,
where he deposits her for the time being in the

keeping of his younger sister, who forthwith communicates with her friends.

All this is very minutely, and it must be admitted,
very vividly related in the different letters of the
persons concerned. The gentleman who thus splen-
didly and effectively makes his entrance upon the scene
is Richardson's "man of true honour," Sir Charles
Grandison, who has just returned to England after
a lengthy visit to the Continent. As may be anticipated, Sir Hargrave, as soon as he can leave his room,
sends him a pressing invitation to repair, with the
proper equipment, to Kensington Gravel-pits. And
here comes in the solution of Richardson's great difficulty. Although he is an expert swordsman, Sir
Charles of course refuses, as duelling is contrary to
his principles. In a long interview with Sir Hargrave's
representative, Mr. Bagenhall; and in a second and
longer meeting with Sir Hargrave and his friends —
a shorthand writer being conveniently present on both
occasions — he justifies his action. He will not draw
his sword upon a challenge, though he will defend himself, if attacked. His life is not his own, much less is
another man's his. He does not regard the so-called
laws of honour; but he owns to the laws of God and
his country. Richardson makes these arguments, which,
in their full exposition, keep the shorthand writer pretty
hard at work, produce a marked effect upon the other
side, who are gradually won over by the elaborate
coolness, courage, and magnanimity of Grandison.
Eventually the penitent and somewhat dilapidated Sir
Hargrave waits upon Miss Byron to entreat her for-
giveness, which she grants; but undeterred by compassion for his damaged good-looks (" I had now and

then a little pity for his disfigured mouth and lip "),
absolutely declines to consider his proposals of marriage — a decision which, in spite of a formal denial,
he is perhaps not unnaturally disposed to attribute to
Miss Byron's liking for her deliverer.

That she has fallen hopelessly in love with Sir
Charles Grandison is in the nature of things. But a
sixth suitor appears upon the scene in the person of
the Earl of D. (with twelve thousand a year), who is
highly recommended by her friends, while Sir Charles
Grandison, though obviously impressed by the beauty
and good qualities of the lady he has rescued, makes
no attempt to improve the occasion, or to respond to
a passion which she, on her side, finds it extremely
difficult to conceal. *Il y a toujours un autre* — as the
proverb says; and the explanation is, that he is practically pre-engaged. When in Italy, he had saved a
certain Barone della Porretta from assassination by
some Brescian bravoes, and had thus grown acquainted
with the noble Porretta family of Bologna, going even
to such lengths as to teach the only daughter English,
with the usual result. The Signorina Clementina della
Porretta (one loves — as Goldsmith says — "to give the
whole name ") had become desperately attached to her
instructor, who was of course too discreet a fine gentleman to show any signs of returning her affection,
especially as he was a Protestant, and his Italian
friends were Roman Catholics. When the state of
their daughter's affections was at last made manifest,
the Porrettas had proposed to him to renounce his
religion, and make certain other concessions which he
could not accept.

As no compromise was found feasible, he quitted

Italy, and Clementina lost her reason in consequence.
All these things, or most of them, he communicates to
Miss Byron at a private interview, when she is visiting
Colnebrook, where she has been previously made aware,
at immeasurable length, and with much needless detail,
of the entire and not wholly worshipful history of the
Grandison family, which history she in her turn
repeats by letter (there are some fifteen on this
theme alone) to her cousin and correspondent, Lucy
Selby. The outcome of Grandison's confidences to
Miss Byron is, that the Porretta family have again
summoned him to a consultation, and the nature of
the summons seems to indicate that, in the state of
their daughter's health, they are prepared to give way
further in order to secure her happiness. So Sir
Charles, as in duty bound, departs for Italy, leaving
Miss Byron in what may undoubtedly be described as
a " delicate distress."

It would be undesirable, if it were not unnecessary,
to imitate here the interminable deliberation with
which all these continental negotiations are carried
out. At last, when, owing to surrenders on both
sides, matters seem tending to a solution adverse to
Miss Byron, Clementina's awakened conscience rather
unexpectedly reminds her that, even if her parents
permit her to marry a heretic, it is her duty to
renounce her love rather than her religion. This
decision she communicates to her suitor in a letter
which M. Texte not unjustly characterises as admirable.
How can she bind her soul to a soul allied to perdi-
tion ? How can she be sure that he will not draw
her after him by love, by sweetness of manner, by
condescending goodness ? In such and similar terms

she announces her determination not to marry, but to take the veil, urging her lover further, with commendable unselfishness, to seek an English bride. Sir Charles, whose behaviour has of course been painfully irreproachable throughout, is consequently free to pay his addresses to Miss Byron. Making a last fruitless, but scrupulously formal, attempt to shake Clementina's resolution, he returns home, and at once devotes all his available energies to his new enterprise. After a " rencounter " with Mr. Greville, whom, as may be anticipated, he adroitly disarms (Sir Hargrave, it may be premised, dies penitent, leaving large legacies to Sir Charles and his wife), and a six-weeks' engagement which takes two volumes to re-count, he is married to Miss Byron. But the story still goes on. Lady Grandison's Italian predecessor reappears on the scene, flying in disguise from an importunate suitor; her family follow; and are all ultimately assembled at Grandison Hall. At the close it is understood that there is to be no cloister, and that Clementina may in due time accept the addresses of her admirer, the Count of Belvedere. Then comes a Postscript, in which Richardson answers objectors to the faultless character of his hero, and vindicates his views on duelling by printing a section of the Articles of War. With all his perfection and imperfection, Sir Charles — we are told — is intended as a pattern, not indeed to be imitated completely, but endeavoured after. And the Postscript winds up with an apposite quotation from Tillotson's sermons, in part of which that " eminent Divine " appears to plagiarise a well-known couplet of George Herbert. " He that aims at the

heavens, which yet he is sure to come short of, is like
to shoot higher than he that aims at a mark within
his reach." [1]

The above is naturally a very imperfect outline of
the *History of Sir Charles Grandison.* Whether he was,
in reality, or whether he would ever be taken for,
the model which Richardson intended him to be, are
questions still in debate, unless indeed they are held
to be unanswerably settled by the fact he has been
almost universally accepted as the popular exponent
of a courtesy which has more of buckram and punctilio
than of genuine benevolence and propriety. But the
modern reader who approaches the book with open
mind — and open eyes — for seven volumes, two of
which might certainly have been spared, are no
summer's-day pastime, will perhaps regard him a little
more indulgently than the critic who dismisses him
impatiently as a self-conscious prig. As his latest
biographer justly remarks, self-consciousness is in-
separable from the analytic method; and Sir Charles
Grandison is not Richardson's solitary sinner in this
kind. Like Carlyle's Monks of Mount Athos, most of
his characters are in the habit of morbidly interro-
gating their internal mechanism. But forgive this, —
forgive the author's constitutional longwindedness, —
forgive the old-fashioned gallantry which requires a hero
("as calls himself a hero") to wipe the tear-drop from
a heroine's cheek, and afterwards to kiss the handker-
chief; — forgive the lapses of a writer depicting by an
effort of imagination a society of which he knew little

[1] " — who aimeth at the sky
Shoots higher much than he that means a tree."
                              The Temple, lvi.

or nothing experimentally : [1] — forgive or forget all these things ; and it is really marvellous how well he has succeeded in his self-imposed task, — how much he has avoided which might have been absurd, — and how interesting upon the whole his hero remains. Recognising that to make him reveal himself too much would be out of character, Richardson has, however, put his praises far too lavishly into the mouths of those about him. And it is these who most offend. Grandison himself is not really so unsupportable : it is the women worshippers (there are half a dozen besides Harriet and Clementina); it is the "led-friends," and parasites, and pensioners, and protégés, who surround and applaud him, like the chamberlains in the French tale, with their monotonous refrain : —

> " Que son mérite est extrême !
> Que de grâces, que de grandeur.
> Ah ! combien Monseigneur
> Doit être content de lui-même."

He is brave, he is generous, he is honourable, he is handsome, and he refuses to dock his horses' tails, — which was certainly advanced humanity. Rectify him

---

[1] He himself admitted this, as we have seen (*ante*, p. 51) ; and upon this point, we may hear his great rival. "I am apt to conceive," says Fielding, in *Tom Jones*, Book xiv. Chap. i., "that one reason why many English writers have totally failed in describing the manners of upper life, may possibly be, that, in reality they know nothing of it." . . . "A true knowledge of the world is gained only by conversation [*i.e.* intercourse], and the manners of every rank must be seen in order to be known." In an admirable paper on "Morals and Manners in Richardson," printed in the *National Review* for November 1889, Mrs. Andrew Lang, with an insight denied to "mere man," has collected and criticised some of Richardson's lapses.

by the considerations above set forth, and the reader who has, in addition, fortitude enough to overcome an excusable repugnance to oppressive superior goodness, will probably be more ready to concur with the Master of Balliol and Mr. Ruskin who admired him, than with the brilliant but unkind M. Hippolyte Taine, who suggested flippantly that he should be canonised and stuffed.

Indeed it may be even contended that he is a greater feat of cleverness than any of the other personages in the book, since none of them — of the women at all events — excel Clarissa and Miss Howe. Despite the praise of Warton, the much-vaunted madness of Clementina is not better done than the mental disorder of Clarissa; and a large portion of Miss Howe goes to equip Miss Byron as well as Miss Charlotte Grandison. There are, we believe, who regard Miss Charlotte Grandison as an amusing person. That she is sprightly and vivacious, there is no doubt. But she is also undeniably ill-mannered, and her rudeness is as incapable of pardon as the villainy of Lovelace. When Lady Mary, commenting on Miss Grandison's failure to distinguish between pert folly and humour — between ill-nature and spirit — says roundly that she should have been treated like a humoursome child, and well whipped, she is expressing an opinion in which, even in her own day, she was by no means alone. For according to Miss Talbot, writing to Miss Carter, the Bishop of Oxford, with whom Miss Talbot was staying,[1] was entirely in agreement with the course proposed. " I do love her

---

[1] Dr. Secker, with whom Miss Talbot lived, was Bishop of Oxford, and Dean of St. Paul's.

[Charlotte]," says Miss Talbot to her friend, " as well
as you do, but I do not think you speak with sufficient
respect of Lord G., and her ladyship [Charlotte again]
richly deserved two or three hearty beatings and kick-
ings which the Bishop of Oxford did most heartily
wish her." That, in any matrimonial alliance, Miss
Grandison's force of character would make her the
predominant partner, is probable; but it is not to
be believed that any husband — even a china-collector
and "fly-catcher " — should have endured her rudeness without reply. " An oak with but one green
leaf on it would have answered her," — as Signor Benedick says. She comes of the same inconceivable stock
as Lady Davers in *Pamela.* Whether there is any
truth in the report that Richardson borrowed some
of her traits from Lady Bradshaigh, it is now difficult
to decide; but at all events it is curious that some of
her most individual expressions are to be found in
Lady Bradshaigh's correspondence; and that Lady
Bradshaigh herself refers " to the saucy freedoms and
impertinences with which she [Lady B.] is too naturally inclined to treat her best friends."

While there is not in *Grandison,* as in *Clarissa,* one
central or dominating event, there is, on the other
hand, no lack of characters destined, for the most
part, to serve as stocks upon which the hero may
exercise his gamut of good qualities. Indeed the
variety and fertility of these subordinates, as well as
the abundance of incident and invention, is most
remarkable, looking to Richardson's continual protests
as to his age, infirmities, and failing powers. Nevertheless, apart from the hero and his "two loves,"
there is none of the other characters — the Selbys,

the Shirleys, the Reeveses, the Beauchamps, and so
forth — who calls clamorously for extended remark,
while of some of the men it must be admitted that
they are but variations, more or less attenuated, of
characters in the earlier books. And here may be
mentioned one of the peculiarities of the Richardson
gallery. While, with others of his rivals, it is difficult
not to identify their characters with living persons,
real or imaginary, it is part of his process of
invention [the above not very manifest exception of
Lady Bradshaigh does but prove the rule] that no
one has seriously sought for any recognisable models
for Clarissa, or Grandison, or Lovelace.[1] Had they
been drawn " from the quick " — as the old designers
put it — such models had not been far to seek. But
they were minted in the author's " study of imagination," and we can no more seek for their prototypes
in actual life than we can seek for the prototypes of
Hamlet and Iago.

As in the case of *Clarissa*, Richardson seems to have
received various criticisms and suggestions in regard
to *Grandison;* and, after his fashion, to have defended
himself in lengthy letters. Two of these, at least, are in
existence in printed form. One, dated March 15, 1754, is
headed " Copy of a Letter to a Lady, who was solicitous
for an additional volume [!] to the History of Sir Charles
Grandison, supposing it ended abruptly ; and expressing
herself desirous to see Sir Charles's Conduct and Behaviour in the Parental Character ; and to know if the

---

[1] There can be nothing in Johnson's suggestion, as reported
in Miss Seward's *Anecdotes* (ii. 223), that Grandison was mod-
elled on Mr. Robert Nelson of the *Festivals and Fasts*, who died
in 1715.

Story were intended to be carried further."[1] Richardson answers in four pages of minute type, and with the
most admirable gravity. The story will not be continued,
he says. As to its ending abruptly, he points out that,
while *Pamela* was supposed to have taken place within
thirty, and *Clarissa* within twenty years of their respective publications, *Sir Charles Grandison* is com-
paratively up to date, or, in less modern phrase, is
brought down "pretty near to the present time"
[1754]. It is, therefore, quite out of the question to
carry the fortunes of the characters further at present,
with any regard to probability. Lady Grandison, for
instance, cannot go to Italy to visit the Porrettas
before her lying-in, — "the heir of Sir Charles Grandison must not be needlessly, or for a compliment,
exposed to dangers and difficulties;" Clementina,
"her malady not returning," cannot marry the Count
of Belvedere for a year, — and so forth. As to the other
characters, he has, he contends, done quite enough
on their behalf. Everybody who deserves well, is rewarded; for the rest, "who cares for them?" With
respect to the portrayal of Sir Charles in the parental
character, he has entered into that subject pretty
largely in *Pamela*, and it is besides easy to see that
Sir Charles would be an excellent father of a family.
"Permit me further to observe," he says finally, "that
the conclusion of a *single story* is indeed generally some
great and decisive event; as a *Death* or a *Marriage:*
But in scenes of life carried down nearly to the present

---

[1] The writer was not alone in this inquiry. "The Gotten-
burg translators" — says Mrs. Barbauld — "sent for the rest of
the work, supposing it incomplete." (*Correspondence*, 1804,
cxxxii.).

M

time, and in which a *variety of interesting characters* is
introduced; all events cannot be decided, unless as
in the History of *Tom Thumb the Great* [Fielding
again!], all the actors are killed in the last scene;
since persons presumed to be still living, must be
supposed liable to the various turns of human affairs.
All that can be expected therefore in such a work, if
its ending is proposed to afford the most complete
scene of felicity of which human life is capable, must
be to leave the principal characters happy, and the rest
with fair prospects of being so."

The other letter is headed—"Answer to a Letter
from a Friend, who had objected to Sir Charles
Grandison's Offer to allow his Daughters by Lady
Clementina, had his Marriage with her taken Effect, to
be educated Roman Catholics." Seeing the marriage
never came to pass even in fiction, it might perhaps be
thought that discussion on this question was superfluous, to say nothing of the fact that in his concluding
Note to the novel, the author had seemed to deprecate,
if not absolutely decline, any controversy of the kind.
But as he received several anonymous letters to the effect
that he should have exposed the iniquity of such compromise, he felt bound (and he was never loth) to make
some reply. His defence, as usual, is not an entirely
satisfactory one, inasmuch as he appears to be opposed
to the compromise suggested. But he points out that
something was surrendered by the other side as well;
and also that, although the circumstances of the case
compelled his hero "to make some concessions, in compassion to an excellent woman, who laboured under a
disorder of mind on his account," his action was not
countenanced by his judgment. Indeed, he implies

that he [Sir Charles] "thought himself not unhappy that a marriage, to be entered into upon such terms, took not effect; as well as that it was owing to Clementina herself, and not to him, that it did not; frequent as such compromises are in marriage-treaties between people of different persuasions." Whether this answer satisfied his correspondents, all of whom were laudably zealous for the interests of the Protestant cause, may be doubted. There is no doubt, however, that Richardson valued himself not a little, as Mrs. Barbauld says, upon his nice conduct of this matter, and particularly upon his liberality to the Catholic religion. One minor point in connection with this letter, is its citation of an expression which was later to become a household word. The phrase, " a Citizen of the World," is as old as Bacon's *Essays;* but it is interesting to find it in Richardson only a few years before Goldsmith made it the title of his collected " Chinese Letters." Sir Charles Grandison, says Lucy Selby, "is, in the noblest sense, a Citizen of the World."

By Richardson's admirers, *Sir Charles Grandison* was welcomed with an applause as great as that accorded to *Pamela* and *Clarissa.* Mr. Urban, reviewing the first four volumes only, but apparently with full knowledge of the whole, while admitting that the events and adventures were few, and that the narrative stood still too long, is eloquent as to their other merits. " All the recesses of the human heart are explored, and its whole texture unfolded. Such a knowledge of the polite world, of men and manners, may be acquired from an attentive perusal of this work as may in a great measure supply the place of the tutor and boarding-school. Young persons may learn how to

act in all the important conjunctures, and how to
behave gracefully, properly, and politely, in all the
common occurrences of life." His private correspondents use stronger language. " I look upon you," says
Dr. Young, who, it must be remembered, was the later
author of *The Centaur not Fabulous,* "as a peculiar
instrument of Providence, adjusted to the peculiar
exigence of the times; in which all would be *fine
gentlemen,* and only are at a loss to know what that
means." Cibber rants as usual, and drags in Pope.
" Since I was born I cannot say, that in all my reading
of ancients and moderns, I ever met with such variety
of entertainment; so much goodness of heart, and so
indefatigable a capacity to give proofs of it. . . . I
had rather have the fame that your amiable zeal for it
[virtue] deserves, than be preferred as a poet to a *Pope,*
or his *Homer.*"[1] "He [Sir Charles] shall be my
master," says Mr. Edwards of Turrick; "and it will
be my own very great fault, if I am not better for his
lessons to the last day of my life." There is much
more to the same effect in other letters, from which it
is manifest that some of Richardson's readers of 1754
did not value their *Grandison* for the story alone.
Perhaps the oddest example of this is contained in a
letter included among the miscellaneous correspondence
at South Kensington, and purporting to come from an

---

[1] Cibber's language is extravagant; but it has been made
worse than it deserves. In one of his letters to Richardson,
of which Mrs. Barbauld prints a *facsimile* in her sixth volume,
he expresses his desire to come "and nibble upon a bit more"
of Miss Byron, upon whom he has already made "a delicious
meal." In the text the printers have substituted for "nibble"
another and less appropriate word, with which he is usually,
and unfairly, credited.

imprisoned debtor. Under date of 2nd May 1754, one " B. F." writes to Richardson to announce his conversion from libertinism, owing to the improving influence of Sir Charles Grandison, and the salutary monition conveyed by the dreadful catastrophe of Sir Hargrave Pollexfen. What five years' incarceration, with all its attendant want and indigence, could not effect, Richardson's "good man" has achieved; and for the future, virtue and honour are to be the standard and governor of all the writer's actions. This ingenuous effusion *may*, of course, have been *bonâ fide*. But, in all probability, it was speedily followed by some liberal gratuity from the fluttered and flattered author, which, as speedily, went the way of that guinea thoughtfully despatched every Monday by his friends to another enforced resident in the Fleet Liberties, Mr. Richard Savage, by whom, as Johnson assures us, it was "commonly spent before the next Morning."

In the first of the two letters upon the subject of Sir Charles Grandison, to which reference has recently been made, Richardson states that the delay in issuing his final volume — a delay which had caused some persons to imagine that " marvellous events, and violent catastrophes, were preparing " — was occasioned " by the treatment I met with from Dublin." He has himself explained these circumstances in a pamphlet issued in September 1753, with the title, *The Case of Samuel Richardson, of London, Printer, on the Invasion of his Property in the History of Sir Charles Grandison, before Publication, by certain Booksellers in Dublin.* He had arranged with George Faulkner, the Dublin Bookseller, and friend of Swift, to take sheets of the work to be set up, and printed in Dublin. He had been warned against possible piracy; but he had, as he imagined, by special injunctions to his foreman and others, taken all reasonable precautions. Nevertheless, by a combination of bribery, negligence, and fraud, during his absence on a brief visit to Bath to bring back his daughter Polly, the sheets of five of the volumes, and parts of the sixth and seventh, were smuggled to Ireland, where an incomplete and un-authorised edition was issued before the book had appeared in London, — the piratical putters-forth being Messrs. Exshaw, Wilson, and Saunders of Dublin. Richardson was highly incensed, and no doubt fretted sadly, as his correspondence shows, over this " Invasion of his Property " by the " Irish Rapparees," for which, however, in the existing state of the law, it was not possible for his friends to offer any consolation but sympathy. He issued the above-mentioned pamphlet, and made various appeals to his Irish correspondents, but without obtaining any redress. Worse than this, he seems to have had reason to apprehend that the same nefarious course would be taken in Scotland, and that pirated copies would be transmitted to France for translation.

Among other persons who commented upon this piece of unjustifiable sharp practice was Arthur Murphy, who, in No. 3 of his new paper, the *Gray's Inn Journal*, and under his assumed character of " Mr. Charles Ranger," made it the text of some very sensible remarks upon the calamities of authors. After referring to these in general, and particularly to that infamous and detestable action for which, " owing to the Poverty of the Language," no stronger term is used than piracy, he goes on — " MR. RICHARDSON,

Author of the celebrated Pamela, and the justly
admired Clarissa (if I may be allowed to judge from
his Productions) is subject to every delicate Sensation
above ascribed to fine Writers, and therefore, after his
having prepared for the Public, *The* History *of* Sir
Charles Grandison, and printed the same entirely
at his own Expence, which cannot but amount to a
large Sum, an ingenuous Mind must be shocked to find,
that Copies of very near all this Work, from which the
Public may reasonable expect both Entertainment and
Instruction, have been clandestinely and fraudulently
obtained by a Set of Booksellers in *Dublin*, who have
printed off the same, and advertised it in the public
Papers, even before the lawful Proprietor has made
Publication here.

"I am not inclined to cast national Reflections, but
I must avow, that I look upon this to be a more
flagrant and atrocious Proceeding than any I have
heard of for a long Time. Wit has been finely called,
'the Owner's Wife, which other Men enjoy,' and, in
this Instance, the Phrase appears to me more just than
ever, as great Part of that Profit, which Mr. *Richardson*
might justly promise himself, is rapaciously seized
from him, and that too, by the vile Artifices of Bribing
the Author's Servants, which is a Practice unworthy
of the meanest Member of the Common-Wealth of
Learning."

The paper concludes with an expression of regret
that the laws of the land have not sufficiently secured
to Authors the property of their works; and by the
issue of a burlesque order from Parnassus, signed by
Jonathan Swift, to the students of Trinity-College,
Dublin, enjoining them to toss Messrs. Exshaw, Wilson,

and Saunders in a blanket, but not till they are dead."
It does not appear that Richardson obtained even this
modest satisfaction for his wrongs; and, though he
afterwards sent a cheap authorised edition of *Sir
Charles* to Ireland, the pirates continued to undersell
him, and he made but scant profit in that island by his
venture.

CHAPTER VII

LAST YEARS AND GENERAL ESTIMATE

Once — in all probability upon that visit to Bath with Mrs. Richardson to which reference was made in the foregoing chapter — the Rev. Richard Graves, Rector of Claverton, and afterwards author of the *Spiritual Quixote*, met the author of *Sir Charles Grandison* at the house of Mr. James Leake, who, it will be remembered, was Richardson's brother-in-law. The interview took place in the bookseller's parlour, which we may, perhaps, fairly assume to have been that pleasant, and still existent, vaulted chamber on the " Walks," close to Lilliput Alley, which was the favoured resort of Fielding's " 'Squire Allworthy," Ralph Allen, and where Sheridan, later, is said to have written *The Rivals*. [1] Richardson told Mr. Graves that he was going to dine with Mr. Allen at Prior Park. " Twenty years ago," said he, " I was the most obscure man in Great Britain, and now I am admitted to the company of the first characters in the Kingdom." His exultation was pardonable, but exaggerated. Many estimable and some distinguished people had recognised his ability, but they scarcely constituted the illustrious body to whom he compared them. " The doors of the Great were

[1] Peach's *Life and Times of Ralph Allen*, 1895, pp. 73, 135.

169

never opened to him," says candid Lady Mary, with whom Mrs. Barbauld is very severe, appealing to the list of Richardson's friends and correspondents as proof to the contrary. But the evidence invoked scarcely supports her contention. It is true that Richardson was occasionlly visited at North End by the Bishop of Oxford (Dr. Secker), and by Lord Trentham — the Sir Thomas Robinson who had been one of the Trustees of the defunct "Society for the Encouragement of Learning." Arthur Onslow, the Speaker, Richardson had known before he began to write. But for his other friends, — Lady Bradshaigh, and Lady Echlin, the Delanys, Mrs. Donnellan, Miss Sutton, Warburton, Allen himself, Young, and so forth, — they can hardly be held to justify the description of them which he has given. That they were friends of a standing greatly superior to that of those he might have expected to make had he continued to be nothing but a Fleet Street printer, and that he was justifiably proud of his relations with them (he gave lavish vails to Onslow's servants to secure their respect) — may be conceded. But the testimony of the mourning rings which he left in his will shows that the roll of his intimates scarcely went beyond his known correspondents; and it must be concluded that Lady Mary was substantially accurate in what she said. Since 1740, however, his general social position had distinctly improved, and his means, without opulence, were easy. His books, though still professedly anonymous, had brought him considerable reputation; and he had, in due course, become Master of the Stationers' Company, — an office, says Mrs. Barbauld, "not only honourable but lucrative," and of which the

sole drawback was the pitiful part which a valetudinarian must play at those full-fed city-feasts of which
Hogarth has given us a glimpse in the eighth plate of
Industry and Idleness. " I cannot but figure to myself"
— writes Thomas Edwards — " the miserable example
you will set at the head of their loaded tables, unless
you have two stout jaw-workers for your wardens,
and a good hungry court of assistants!"

This letter is dated 20th November 1754. A week
or two earlier, Richardson, much to the dismay of his
" worthy-hearted wife," had moved from his comfortable
house at North End to the new suburban residence at
Parson's Green of which mention was made in Chapter
v. The reasons for this appear to have been imperative.
His old landlord, Samuel Vanderplank, had died in
1749; and the property was now in the hands of a
Mr. Pratt. Mr. Vanderplank, who had two daughters
with good expectations, was apparently as alive as was
Richardson in the *Familiar Letters* to the dangers likely
to arise from the " *clandestine* Addresses of *Fortune-
hunters* "; and occupying, as he did, the other half of
the Grange, was not ill-pleased to have for neighbour
and tenant, at a low rent, a man who was at once a
moralist, and a married man without sons. But Mr.
Pratt, to whom Mr. Vanderplank's estate passed from
his son-in-law, Mr. Gilbert Jodrell, was of a different
temper. Not only did he propose to raise the rent
from £25 to £40 a year; but he declined to make any
allowance for the improvements which Richardson had
effected, among which, it has been suggested, the
famous grotto should perhaps have been included.
From another source we learn that the transfer to
Parson's Green, in alterations to the house and garden,

cost Richardson £300, so that, at his advanced age, it
would almost seem as if it might have been more
economical in the end to have remained where he was
even at a rental of double his original amount. But he
had doubtless, in too great perfection, the Englishman's
dislike to being taken at a disadvantage, to make any
minute calculation in the matter; and in October 1754
he quitted North End, which had been his home for
sixteen years, or the whole of his literary life.
"Richardson is very busy," writes Mrs. Delany, under
date of the 30th, "removing this very day to Parson's
Green. Dr. Delany called yesterday at Salisbury
Court." On the 26th of the following month, he is in
residence. "The Speaker was so good as to call upon
me at Parson's Green. He liked the house and situation." And Mrs. Richardson is becoming reconciled to
the change. "She and her girls have been settled in
the new habitation for near a month past; and like it
better and better, as they declare, every day." Then
comes a later letter in December. "She [Mrs. Richard-
son], as you foretold, likes her removal to Parson's
Green every day more and more."

The new house, which was in reality an old house,
since, as far back as 1679, it had been the residence of
a subsequent Lord Chief-Justice of the King's Bench,
Sir Edmund Saunders, is now no longer in existence,
having been pulled down early in the last century.
According to the *Ambulator* for 1800, it stood "at the
corner of the Green," west of Peterborough House, on
a site which, when Brayley wrote, sixteen years later,
corresponded with that of the house terminating Pitt's
Peace, now Arragon House [247 New King's Road],
but then occupied as an academy by Dr. James Taylor.

It lay consequently, as Richardson describes it, on the
road to Fulham, Putney, and Richmond. In 1779 it
was sketched and engraved by J. P. Malcolm, of
Chalton Street, Somers Town, who calls it in his title
"The House at Fulham in which Richardson wrote
Clarissa." [1] As to Fulham, he was right, for Parson's
Green, like North End, was in Fulham Parish ; but as
to *Clarissa*, he was manifestly wrong, since *Clarissa* had
not only been written but published many years before.
Malcolm's print shows the porch from which Richardson
was prepared to welcome the passing stranger. Whether
the North End grotto, or any part of it, found its way
to the new residence, cannot be affirmed. Mme. de
Genlis, who, many years afterwards, visited Richardson's son-in-law, Mr. Bridgen, in order to inspect a
portrait of the novelist, was shown in Mr. Bridgen's
garden a seat on which Richardson had been accustomed to sit and compose, the right arm of which
opened, and held an inkstand. This undoubtedly
suggests the seat at North End which Mr. Erasmus
Reich of Leipzig is declared to have embraced in his
enthusiasm. "I kissed the ink-horn on the side of it,"
says the perfervid gentleman from Saxony. It may
be that the fittings of the North End summer-house,
which was one of Richardson's "improvements," found
their way to Parson's Green; and thus the artless
poem which appears in the fifth volume of Dodsley's
Collection (1763) becomes intelligible. It is headed
Upon an Alcove, now at Parson's *Green*, and consists
of eight verses of which the following are two and
seven : —

[1] There is also a woodcut of it by M. U. Sears, after an old
drawing, in the *Saturday Magazine* for 22nd June 1839.

" Here the soul-harr'wing genius form'd
    His PAMELA's enchanting story !
And here divine CLARISSA died
    A martyr to our sex's glory !

" Here GRANDISON, to crown the whole,
    A bright exemplar stands confest !
Who stole those virtues we admire
    From the great Author's glowing breast."

"Our sex" — betrays the female pen; and, as a
matter of fact, the author is revealed in later editions
of Dodsley as Mrs. Bennet, Mr. Bridgen's sister. There
can therefore be little doubt that the " sacred seat "
thus celebrated was the one which Mr. Reich had kissed,
and which Mr. Bridgen exhibited to Mme. de Genlis.
It may be added here that, in the Parson's Green house,
died Richardson's correspondent, Thomas Edwards.
This was in January 1757. It has been suggested that
one of Richardson's reasons for fixing upon Parson's
Green as a place of residence was to be nearer Fulham
Church. He certainly had a pew there, No. 7 in the
North Gallery. But his horror of a crowd has already
been referred to ; and his growing nervous disorders
probably made him, at all events in his latter years,
a sparing and infrequent worshipper.

The removal to Parson's Green, as we have seen,
was by no means an inexpensive one. But, in the
following year, the house in Salisbury Court was
announced to be unsafe, and it became necessary to
seek some securer premises. " The house I live in,"
he tells Lady Bradshaigh's sister, Lady Echlin, in
December 1755, "in Salisbury Court, has been ad-
judged to have stood near its time: and my very
great printing weights at the top of it, have made it

too hazardous for me to renew an expiring lease. I
have taken a building lease of a court of houses, eight
in number, which were ready to fall; have pulled
them down, and on new foundations, have built a
most commodious printing-office; and fitted up an
adjoining house, which I before used as a warehouse,
for the dwelling-house." If he had named the "court
of houses, eight in number," it might have saved
trouble to his biographers. The "adjoining house"
to which he moved stood in the north-west corner of
the present square, and upon the authority of succes-
sive editions of Cunningham's *London*, it has generally
been stated that the offices were in Blue Ball Court,
now Bell's Buildings, on the eastern side. But, in
a codicil to his will dated July 1760, he speaks of
his offices at that date as being in White Lyon Court,
which lies to the north of the north-west corner, and
was entered from Fleet Street between the existing
Salisbury Court and Whitefriars Street, — that old
Water Lane where, at the sign of the Harrow,
dwelt Goldsmith's long-suffering tailor, William Filby.
White Lyon Court may fairly be said to "adjoin"
the new house, which could scarcely be affirmed of the
houses in Blue Ball Court. However commodious
the new premises were, the new house was neither so
pleasant nor so airy as the old — at least so thought
Mrs. Richardson. "Everybody," her husband told
Lady Bradshaigh, "is more pleased with what I have
done than my wife." But when he wrote, the had
not seen it; and perhaps grew reconciled to it rapidly,
as she had done to the change to Parson's Green.
Where his first house stood, it is not easy to say. A
correspondent, quoted by Mrs. Barbauld, who visited

him about 1753, says it was in the centre of the
square, which is not very definite, although it may
be safely concluded that this could not accurately
describe a house in a corner, though it might a
house in the middle of a row. In any case, his
first house has long disappeared, while the house
that he moved to in 1755 has now given place to
Lloyd's Printing-offices.

The Salisbury Court alterations cost him some
£1400; and from the letter which tells us this, we
also learn that, at this date, his weekly expenses to
journeymen, etc., were from £30 to £40, and that,
in March 1756, his bill for printing the House of
Commons Journals was still unpaid. Not many tradi-
tions linger about Salisbury Court beyond the well-
known one that he used sometimes to hide a half-crown
among the types in order to reward the early bird
among his workmen; and that, owing to his increasing
nervousness, and the impenetrable deafness of his foreman, Mr. Tewley, he gradually came to issue all his
orders in writing. It is usually to this date (1756–57)
that is assigned the story of his employing Goldsmith
as a reader or corrector of the press — Goldsmith, it is
said, having been recommended to his notice by a
disabled master printer whom he was attending in
his brief experience as a Bankside doctor. Of this
employment there is a certain confirmation, though
not a very direct one, in an anecdote related by one
of Goldsmith's Edinburgh acquaintance, Dr. Farr.
Goldsmith, says this gentleman, called upon him when
in London one morning before he was up, dressed "in
a rusty full-trimmed black suit," with the pockets
stuffed with papers like the poet in Garrick's *Lethe*.

He promptly produced part of a manuscript tragedy which he forthwith began to read to his friend, hastily obliterating whatever was objected to. At last he let out that he had already submitted what he had written to Mr. Richardson, whereupon his hearer, alarmed for the fate of a possible masterpiece, " peremptorily declined offering another criticism upon the performance." It is to this period in Richardson's life, too, that we must assign the familiar story of his timely aid to Johnson in durance. Johnson, who was ailing, wrote to him from Gough Square, entreating his assistance, being, he said, " under an arrest for five pounds eighteen shillings." Strahan and Millar were not attainable, so he appealed to Richardson, who at once despatched the money, docketing the application, in his usual business-like way, — " March 16, 1756. Sent six guineas. Witness, Wm. Richardson," — William Richardson being the nephew and assistant of whom we shall hear later in connection with his will. Arthur Murphy, who printed Johnson's letter from the original then before him (it had previously appeared in the *Gentleman's Magazine* for June 1788), is virtuously indignant as to the fact that the remittance only exceeded the request by eight shillings. " Had an incident of this kind occurred in one of his Romances, Richardson would have known how to grace his hero; but in fictitious scenes generosity costs the writer nothing." This is not quite fair. Johnson, as an earlier letter shows, had already made demands upon Richardson; and although, as far as we are aware, he never repeated his application, Richardson could have had no means of knowing whether he was going to become a chronic borrower — a fact which surely

N

justifies him in complying literally with the application
made to him.

After *Grandison*, Richardson essayed no further work
of fiction. His friends, of course, called eagerly for
more. Would he not give them a *bad* woman as a
set-off to his good woman? Then the Widow, — the
Widow was yet unattempted. "I wish to see an
exemplary widow drop from your pen," writes Lady
Echlin; "a very wicked widow has appeared in print
lately. An amiable character would be an agreeable
contrast; it would shine brightly after that black she-
monster, the abominable *Widow of the Wood*" — this
last being a scandalous pamphlet by Benjamin Victor,
the Irish laureate and theatrical manager, dealing incidentally with several well-known Staffordshire families,
who hastily bought it up. But although Richardson
was never well when he had not a pen in his hand,
and, according to Miss Talbot, would have given a good
deal to be fairly got into the midst of a new work, he
was not attracted by these suggestions, or by the
further proposition that he should try his hand at a
Play. He continued, as before, to correspond at
enormous length with his friends, of whom many
still remained to him. Among epistles not hitherto
enumerated, the South Kensington collection contains
a series, also not included in Barbauld, from Aaron
Hill's married daughter, Urania Johnson, now a widow,
and apparently a very necessitous one. It extends
from 1750 to 1758. Richardson seems to have done
what he could for her both by money gifts and by
written recommendations. Urania was the most literary
of the three sisters of Plaistow; and when we hear of
her for the last time, she has submitted a manuscript

novel called *Almira* to the author of *Pamela* and *Clarissa* which that incorruptible critic has been obliged
to censure for lack of delicacy—an objection which
was, of course, most unwillingly received. Another
unpublished "admirer," who occupies a considerable
portion of two of the Forster folios, is a Warwick
attorney, one Eusebius Sylvester.[1] Mr. Sylvester is
"B. F." of the Fleet "writ large." He begins by
flattery and applications for moral counsel. These
latter eventually take the form of requests for pecun-
iary aid, which Richardson rather unwillingly gives,
as loans, tempered by advice, and the final non-pay-
ment of the money brings the correspondence to an
angry and undignified termination. This Sylvester
episode exhibits Richardson at his best and at his
weakest, by showing how readily his native benevolence became the dupe of his morbid appetite for
what, upon this occasion, he comes to qualify bitterly
as the "undesired and officious Applause of his Writings," forgetting that in his earliest communication he
had welcomed it as "kind and generous Approbation." The spectacle is scarcely edifying; but it is
by no means uncommon.

After the publication of his novels, Richardson had
many foreign correspondents. To Pastor John Stinstra,
who translated *Clarissa* into Dutch, reference has
already been made. Another correspondent was
Erasmus Reich, the Leipzig librarian, who had visited
him at North End; and a third, Gellert the fabulist,

---

[1] Curiously enough, there is a Mr. Sylvester, "a worthy
attorney," in *Sir Charles Grandison*. But the real Sylvester does
not seem to have known Richardson until August 1754, after
Grandison was published. Richardson refers to this odd
coincidence in his first letter to his new friend.

who translated *Pamela* and *Grandison*, over which
latter work, and *Clarissa*, according to his own confes-
sion, he had "wept away some of the most remarkable
hours of his life, in a sort of delicious misery." But the
most interesting of this group is Mrs. Klopstock, the
young and not-long-wedded wife of the author of
the *Messiah* who first wrote to Richardson in 1757.
Apparently he had heard much of her husband through
a certain Major Hohorst, who had visited North End,
and composed an *Ode on the death of Clarissa*. As "the
single young girl," she says, in her pretty broken
English, she had not dared to write to the novelist;
but as the wife of Klopstock, she thinks she may, and
she does. Her first letter, which is also her first letter
in English ("French is too *fade* a language to use"), is
dated 29th November, and is written to thank him for
Clarissa and *Grandison*. She had wanted him to write
"a *manly* [male?] Clarissa," and he has written one in
Grandison. "Now you can write no more, you must
write the history of an Angel." Richardson replies by
asking her for the brief history of her attachments, her
pursuits, her alliances. He wishes "to know everything a relation would wish to know of his dear Hamburg kindred." Thereupon she rejoins — "You will
know all what concerns me. Love, dear Sir, is all
what me concerns! And love shall be all what I will
tell you in this letter." One happy night she had read
the *Messiah* (she writes), and next day was informed
by one of Klopstock's friends that it was by Klopstock.
"I believe, I fell immediately in love with him. At
the least, my thoughts were ever with him filled,
especially because his friend told me very much of his
character." But she had no hopes of ever seeing him,

until she heard, quite unexpectedly, that he would pass through Hamburg. Upon this, she wrote immediately to Klopstock's friend "for procuring by his means that she might see the author of the *Messiah*, when in Hamburg." The result was that Klopstock called upon her. "I must confess," she goes on, "that, though greatly prepossessed of his qualities, I never thought him the amiable youth whom I found him. This made its effect. After having seen him two hours, I was obliged to pass the evening in a company, which never had been so wearisome to me. I could not speak, I could not play; I thought I saw nothing but Klopstock. I saw him the next day, and the following, and we were very seriously friends. But the fourth day he departed. It was a strong hour the hour of his departure! He wrote soon after, and from that time our correspondence began to be a very diligent one. I sincerely believed my love to be friendship. I spoke with my friends of nothing but Klopstock, and showed his letters. They raillied at me, and said I was in love. I raillied them again, and said they must have a very friendshipless heart, if they had no idea of friendship to a man as well as to a woman. Thus it continued eight months, in which time my friends found as much love in Klopstock's letters as in me. I perceived it likewise, but I would not believe it. At last Klopstock said plainly, that he loved, and I startled as for a wrong thing. I answered, that it was no love, but friendship, as it was what I felt for him; we had not seen one another enough to love (as if love must have more time than friendship!)" A year after they had first seen each other, Klopstock came again to Hamburg, and the letter proceeds — "We saw, we were friends, we

loved; and we believed that we loved; and a short
time after I could even tell Klopstock that I loved."
But they had still to wait two years. Her mother, a
widow, could not agree to let her marry a stranger. At
last the mother relented. "We married, and I am the
happiest wife in the world. In some few months it
will be four years that I am so happy, and still I dote
upon Klopstock as if he were my bridegroom." A
subsequent letter gives a picture of their married life;
— the progress of his poem (now past its tenth book)
and of which she knows most, "being always present
at the birth of the young verses!" "You may think
that persons who love as we do, have no need of two
chambers; we are always in the same," — she sitting at
her needle, very still and quiet, while her husband, with
rapt face, composes his hexameters. Then he reads
her his "young verses," by which she no doubt means
his first draught, and "suffers her criticisms." In a
third letter her only wish ungratified for four years
seems likely to be realised; she is expecting to become
a mother. Klopstock has gone on a visit to Copen-
hagen, and they write to each other every post. But
she will speak no more of this little cloud of separation;
she will only tell her happiness. "A son of my dear
Klopstock! Oh, when shall I have him! It is long
since I have made the remark, that geniuses do not
engender geniuses. No children at all, bad sons, or
at the most, lovely daughters, like you and Milton.
But a daughter or a son, only with a good heart, without genius, I will nevertheless love dearly." . . . "When
I have my husband and my child, I will write you more
(if God gives me health and life)." But it was not to
be; and the next letter, a brief note from a Hanover

correspondent, announces her death in childbirth. Her husband, who wrote her epitaph, survived her for forty-six years, and only married again very late in life, in order to give a kinswoman, who lived with him, a widow's claim to the different pensions he enjoyed.

The remainder of Richardson's life presents few incidents of interest. The only work of any importance, hitherto unmentioned, which he produced was the volume entitled *A Collection of the Moral and Instructive Sentiments, Maxims, Cautions, and Reflexions, contained in the Histories of Pamela, Clarissa, and Sir Charles Grandison. Digested under proper Heads, with References to the Volume, and Page, both in Octavo and Twelves, in the respective Histories.* It is sometimes supposed that this was prompted by a request of Johnson,—a supposition which is erroneous. When the fourth, or 1751, edition of *Clarissa* came out, it was only provided with a selection of the " Moral and Instructive Sentiments " which it contained; and Johnson pressed in addition for an *index rerum*, which would enable the reader to find readily any incident to which he desired to refer. It was probably in response to his suggestion, which was renewed when Johnson received the early volumes of *Sir Charles Grandison*, that that novel was provided, not only with a table of the " Similies, and Allusions," but with a closely-packed " Index Historical and Characteristical " of more than one hundred pages. In the volume of which the title is above transcribed, the moral and instructive element comes again to the front, and the book includes little or no information as to the characters or occurrences in the stories. As a *pensée*-writer, Richardson cannot rank either with Pascal or Vauvenargues,—indeed the very qualities of

his style preclude him from presenting his thoughts
with gnomic precision; but there is naturally much
plain sense in his utterances, and the fervent Richardsonian would have no difficulty in constructing a selection of respectable, if rather trite, aphorisms from
his four hundred pages.

Here are a few dispersed specimens : —

"Great men do evil, and leave it to their Flatterers
to find a reason for it afterwards."

" True Generosity is more than Politeness, it is more
than good Faith, it is more than Honour, it is more
than Justice ; since all these are but duties."

"People who find their anger has made them considerable, will seldom be pleased."

"Great sentiments uttered with dignity by a good
person, gives, as it were, a visibility to the soul."

"The art of governing the under-bred lies more in
looks than in words."

" The lower class of people are ever aiming at the
stupid wonderful."

" Persons who by their rashness have made a breach in
their duty, should not enlarge it by their impatience."

"To reform by an enemy's malevolence, is the
noblest revenge in the world."

"He that would act more greatly than a prince,
may, before he is aware, be less than a gentleman."

" Extraordinary merit has some forfeitures to pay."

All but the last two of the above are taken from
Clarissa. Here is an astounding one from *Pamela :* —

" It is not beneath a person of the highest quality to
visit and comfort one of low degree, who is contending

with sickness, or who is struggling in the pangs of death."

At the end of the book to which is prefixed a Preface " by a Friend " (Warburton), Richardson reprinted the two letters about Grandison of which an account was given in the previous chapter.

In 1757 his eldest daughter, Mary, was married to Mr. Philip Ditcher, a respectable surgeon at Bath, whose acquaintance she had no doubt made upon that visit to Nash's city, from which, four years before, her parents had fetched her back at the time of the Dublin piracies. It was a good match; though Richardson grumbled a little, partly, it seems, because Miss Polly had consoled herself for the loss of an old love rather more expeditiously than was seemly in her father's daughter. " Mr. Ditcher's Task was as easy as he could wish : Too easy, I think, between you and me, considering another affair was so recently gone off," says a letter to Mrs. Chapone in June 1758. But nothing much could really be offered in the way of objection. "He [Richardson] now," writes Mrs. Barbauld, " allowed himself some relaxation from business; and only attended from time to time, his printing-offices in London. He often regretted that he had only females to whom to transfer his business; however, he had taken in to assist him a nephew [this was the William Richardson who witnessed the loan to Johnson], who relieved him from the more burdensome cares of it, and who eventually succeeded him." Three years after Polly's marriage, he entered into partnership with Miss Catherine Lintot, only daughter and heiress of Henry Lintot, son of Pope's publisher. Miss

Lintot was another of the young ladies to whom, from one of his letters to her, he seems to have stood *in loco parentis*, and he purchased a moiety of her Patent of Law Printer to the King, an arrangement which necessitated the transfer of Miss Lintot's share of the business from the Savoy to Richardson's premises in White Lyon Court. He was now comfortably off, and able to make provision for his family. But he was no longer young, being in fact over seventy, besides being enfeebled by obscure nervous disorders, and a life of prolonged application. Apparently, also, he suffered from insomnia. "Bad Rest is my Misfortune and makes my Days unhappy," he tells Mrs. Chapone. "Sad, sad, writing! a Course of terrible Nights!" he says again in the above-mentioned letter to Miss Lintot, which is dated September 1759. In July 1761 he was attacked by apoplexy. His illness is thus referred to in a letter from Miss Talbot to Mrs. Carter : — "Poor Mr. Richardson was seized on Sunday evening with a most severe paralytic stroke. . . . It sits pleasantly upon my mind, that the last morning we spent together was particularly friendly, and quiet, and comfortable. It was the 28th of May — he looked then so well! One has long apprehended some stroke of this kind; the disease made its gradual approaches by that heaviness which clouded the cheerfulness of his conversation, that used to be so lively and so instructive ; by the encreased tremblings which unfitted that hand so peculiarly formed to guide the pen ; [1]

---

[1] "For years before his death," says Mrs. Barbauld, "he could not lift the quantity of a small glass of wine to his mouth, though put into a tumbler, without assistance" (*Corr.* 1804, I. clxxx.).

and by, perhaps, the querulousness of temper, most
certainly not natural to so sweet and so enlarged a
mind, which you and I have lately lamented, as
making his family at times not so comfortable as
his principles, his study, and his delight to diffuse
happiness wherever he could, would otherwise have
done." This letter was written on the 2nd July. On
the 4th Richardson died at Parson's Green, and was
buried in the central aisle of St. Bride's (where also
lies his famous predecessor, Wynkyn de Worde), by
the side of his first wife, Martha Wilde. His tomb-
stone, which records the burial of several other
members of his family, is near the pulpit. There is
also a brass mural tablet in the church, erected to
his memory in 1889 by a member of the Court of
the Stationers' Company.

His will, which was made in 1757 upon the marriage
of his daughter Mary, is a characteristic production,
very lengthy, and having four codicils. By some unaccountable lapse it was misdated 1727, an error which
had of course to be rectified by deposition. Two of the
witnesses were Miss Lintot, then about one-and-twenty,
and Henry Campbell, no doubt the grown-up little boy,
who had exhibited so precocious an appreciation of
Pamela. The funeral was to be "frugally performed."
The expenses were not to exceed £30 to his family, and
he was to be "interred [if the circumstances permitted]
with the remains of his late excellent wife Martha."
Besides the mourning rings already mentioned, there
were bequests to the children of his brothers Benjamin
and William, for whom he had probably always been
the rich man of the family. His widow was one of the
Executors, her brother Allington and Andrew Millar

being two of the others,[1] and his estate was divided
between his wife and unmarried daughters, Mrs.
Richardson taking a third and the daughters two-
thirds.   There are some irritable references to his
nephew William, who, when the will was made, was
acting as his uncle's overseer, though not, apparently,
to his uncle's satisfaction.   Between 1757 and 1759
William Richardson seems to have set up for himself,
and a codicil of the latter year revokes a small bequest
in his behalf, while in a further codicil of the following
year he is mentioned as a " partial and selfish young
man," who had shown " a strong disposition to take
care of himself."   This last codicil refers vaguely to
two special acts of rashness on the part of the mis-
guided William, but in the absence of detail, it is
impossible to form any opinion as to the measure of
his culpability.   Whatever it was, it must have been
condoned, since it is quite clear from Nichols that
he succeeded his uncle in the printing-office.   Nichols
also says (*Anecdotes*, 1812, iv. 581 *n.*) that William
Richardson issued Proposals for a " correct, uniform,
and beautiful " edition of his uncle's novels, together
with some hitherto unpublished letters " on moral
and entertaining subjects."   It was to be in twenty
volumes, *octavo*, at four shillings the volume.   But the
project came to nothing ; and in 1811 was rendered
needless by the appearance of the edition in nineteen
volumes prepared by the Rev. Edward Mangin of

[1] Andrew Millar is conjectured to have been the bookseller indicated by Johnson as " being so habitually and equably drunk,
that his intimate friends never perceived that he was more
sober at one time than another." If this be so, it is surely odd
that Richardson, of all people in the world, should have
selected him for his executor.

Bath. A selection of the Correspondence had already been issued in 1804 by Mrs. Barbauld.

In attempting some picture of Richardson's character, it will be well to take his best qualities first. He was undoubtedly a well-meaning man, diligent, laborious, punctual, methodical, very honourable, very benevolent, very rigid in his principles, and also very religious. He had, in fact, all the traditional virtues of the " Complete English Tradesman " ; and had he died at fifty, would have deserved no better epitaph, — although to his obituary notice it might have been added, as a supplementary merit, that he was " particularly Esteem'd by his Friends as a Master of the Epistolary Style, and Noted for his singular Excellence as an Index Maker." But his deferred literary successes, while they disclosed and developed his latent genius, also developed and disclosed some other less worshipful traits in his disposition. The gradual preoccupation with his work, which was a consequence of his peculiarly introspective method, eventually became an absorbing egotism which at last left him little else to think about; and an absorbing egotism passes easily into inordinate vanity. Added to this, his imperfect education and unlettered life had left him profoundly diffident as to the scope of his own powers, making it necessary that he should be periodically reassured as to those powers by fresh applications of flattery, and flattery, like some other dangerous stimulants, has generally to be administered in increasing doses. Johnson, who respected the purity of his motives, admitted his good qualities, and was under obligations to him besides, bears the strongest testimony to this foible in his friend. Richardson, he later told Mrs.

Piozzi, " could not be contented to sail down the
stream of reputation, without longing to taste the
froth from every stroke of the oar." (The mixed metaphor should no doubt be laid to the credit of the lady
narrator.) "He died" — said Johnson again — "merely
for want of change among his flatterers; he perished
for want of more, like a man obliged to breathe the
same air till it is exhausted." With the growth of
his appetite for praise, grew his impatience of contemporary authors of any eminence. Sterne, Pope,
Fielding — were all systematically depreciated by the
man who professed that he had not read, or could
not read them. Yet he found no difficulty in warmly
commending the poetry of Young and Aaron Hill,
and the prose of Orrery and Thomas Edwards. In
Fielding's case, it is true that he had some definite
ground for personal antipathy. But — as already
hinted — he seems to have been far less affected by
the ridicule cast upon *Pamela* by *Joseph Andrews*,
than annoyed by the success of *Clarissa's* rival, *Tom
Jones*. An adversary he could treat with contempt,
real or feigned; what he could not tolerate was a
popular competitor, and he showed his irritation, it
must be confessed, in a very pitiful fashion. It has
been urged — and should be remembered — that he may
really have felt a genuine distaste for the moral tone
of some of his more illustrious contemporaries ; but
the contention would have more force had he
not been a writer himself. Another characteristic,
traceable to his early training and unexpected
elevation, is a certain note of uneasy servility —
where rank and riches are concerned. This crops
up continually in his correspondence, always with

unpleasant effect. For the rest, a great deal must be allowed to the valetudinarian habit, which prompted him to soften the asperities of his daily life as much as possible, to avoid unnecessary friction, and to break the blow of care. " His perpetual study," says Johnson once more, " was to ward off petty inconveniencies, and procure petty pleasures." These are not the ambitions of a strong-minded, self-reliant man; but they are intelligible, nay, to some extent excusable, in one, no longer young, who had worn himself out by a long course of mechanical drudgery, and then cultivated his constitutional nervousness to the verge of disease by the persistent exercise of a preternaturally minute imaginative faculty. One can conceive that male companions, and especially male companions of a robust and emphatic kind, would have been wholly unsuited to such a nature, which found its fitting atmosphere and temperature in the society of women, refined enough to be appreciative, fastidious enough to be judiciously critical, but above all, ready and willing to supply him, as occasion required, with that fertilising medium of caressing and respectful commendation without which it was impossible for him to make any satisfactory progress with his work.

There are several portraits of Richardson — the majority by Joseph Highmore. Two of these are in the National Portrait Gallery — one to the waist, the other a small full-length, which was painted in 1750,[1] when he was sixty-one. It represents a mild-looking, smooth-cheeked, ruddy-faced, little man in a comfortable flaxen wig, holding his right hand in his bosom

[1] A copy of the head from this portrait was engraved by James Basire in the *Gentleman's Magazine* for September 1792.

(an habitual attitude), and having a letter in his left. There is an earlier (?) picture at Stationers' Hall, which exhibits him with a book. Here he wears a claret-coloured coat, and a somewhat fuller wig. In both the half-length portraits, there is a chair in the background which, like the seat at Parson's Green, has an ink-pot let into the arm, which ink-pot is decorated by a goose quill of formidable dimensions. There is another portrait of Richardson by Highmore, which was painted for Lady Bradshaigh, and is said to be still in the possession of her family, while at Stationers' Hall there is also a picture of Richardson's second wife, a pleasant, dark-eyed woman in a low dress and blue scarf. Hogarth is also credited with a portrait of the novelist. But his most characteristic presentment is surely that by Mason Chamberlin. In this he is shown in the velvet cap he wore in the Grotto, sitting with crossed legs, and having in his hand the little board whereon he was accustomed to prepare those *quarto* pages of correspondence of which there are so many specimens at South Kensington, and which, when finished, were handed to Patty or William to transcribe. To complete the list of portraits, it should be added that in 1901 a bust of Richardson by Mr. George Frampton, A.R.A., was placed in the St. Bride Foundation Institute in Fleet Street, which has been described as standing almost on the very spot where the novelist lived and worked.

Of his first wife, Martha Wilde, who died long before he attained to fame as a writer, we know little or nothing beyond what has been already recorded. Of Elizabeth Leake, her successor, there are naturally fuller details. The second Mrs. Richardson seems to have been a prim, home-keeping, methodical personage, very precise in the performance of her household duties, strict in the management of her daughters, excellent at conserves, and copious in her curtsies. Probably she was a little overpowered by the gushing " garden of ladies " who gathered about her husband in his latter years, and may conceivably have felt a plain woman's misgivings about the genuineness of the feminine admirers who wrote such long and laudatory letters. But though there is evidence to prove that Richardson fidgeted and fretted a little under her formal arrangements and love of management, there is nothing to show that she neglected to be amiable to his friends, or that she did not associate herself entirely with his good deeds and abundant hospitalities. Miss Thomson prints a pretty letter in which Richardson presents his " dear Bet " with a copy of *Clarissa,* and apologises for the unavoidable claims which that lady's history had made upon his attention, to the detriment of their domestic relations. Mrs. Richardson continued to reside at Parson's Green after her husband's death. In February 1771 she issued an advertisement in the *Gazetteer and New Daily Advertiser* denying his connection with a novel called *The History of Sir William Harrington.* Two years afterwards, in November 1773, she died, aged seventy-seven ; her end, according to Mrs. Chapone, having been hastened by the sudden death, at Parson's Green, of one of her married daughters when on a visit there. In accordance with a wish expressed in her will, she was buried by her husband at St. Bride's.

Of Richardson's five daughters, four survived him,

o

— Mary, or Polly, who, as already mentioned, married
Mr. Ditcher of Bath, and died a widow in 1783;
Martha, or Patty, married in 1762 to Mr. Edward
Bridgen, a London merchant; Sarah, married in 1764
to Mr. Crowther, a surgeon of Boswell Court; and
Anne, or Nancy, whose delicate health had caused her
parents much uneasiness, but who, nevertheless, survived the rest of the family to die unmarried in
December 1803, just before the publication of the
Barbauld correspondence.   Mrs. Bridgen died 13th
February 1785, so that the married daughter who died
at Parson's Green in 1773, if Mrs. Chapone be correct,
must have been Mrs. Crowther.   When *Sir Charles
Grandison* was published, Mary, the eldest, was only
twenty, so that they can have been little more than
children during the period of their father's greatest
literary activity; and the report, once current, that
Patty assisted him in the production of *Clarissa*, is
sufficiently negatived by the fact that she was only
twelve when *Clarissa* was published.   Later, however,
she seems to have been his favoured amanuensis.
According to her husband, she not only duly answered
the letters of Richardson's foreign correspondents, but
also replied to many of those in England.   " She wrote
with great judgment, refined sentiment, and in a style
remarkably correct and elegant." [1]   Another favoured
secretary was Anne, but they were all occasionally
enlisted.   They were very carefully brought up by
their parents, who had pronounced views on domestic

[1] This is practically confirmed by Mrs. Klopstock, who begs
Richardson, if writing is incommodious to him, " to dictate
only to Mrs. Patty," who, as she has been told by Major
Hohorst, " writes as [like] her father."

discipline; and perhaps on this account, as well as because of their youth, appear never to have held quite the same position with their father as the literary friends of their own sex, and the numerous adopted children whom he distinguished from the heirs of his body as the "daughters of his mind." "My girls are shy little fools," he said; but it is not improbable that, with all his insight into female character, he lacked the gift of putting them at their ease. It is probable, also, that, for many years, they could never have had much prolonged intercourse with the parent whom they saw only at meals, addressed as "Honour'd Sir," and who, when he was not actually ill, was either working at his business, or writing in his study.

Of Richardson's work, much, of necessity, has already been said in the three chapters of this book which are respectively devoted to his three novels; and, in this place, it only remains to add some general remarks upon this subject, as well as upon the nature and character of his influence upon the writers who followed him both in this country and abroad. As to his work, it would be idle to pretend that lapse of time has not robbed it of much of its early prestige, and brought into stronger light those initial defects which, in its first novelty, were overlooked or condoned. "No one" — wrote Fielding — "will contend that the epistolary Style is in general the most proper to a Novelist"; and what Fielding said in 1747 has been endorsed by the great majority of his successors in the art of fiction. Then Richardson's extraordinary diffuseness and inordinate prolixity, both of which peculiarities were fully recognized by his contemporaries and by himself, must be allowed to be graver disadvantages than ever to-day, when, with the headlong hurry of life, the language of literature seems to tend less towards expansion and leisurely expression than towards the cultus of the short-cut and the snap-shot. And besides these drawbacks of manner and method, there is the further difficulty that the author, who has been handed down to posterity as the first of our domestic novelists, persisted in regarding himself primarily as a moralist and preacher, and, to this end, burdened his text with a mass of matter didactic and hortatory, which, despite Johnson's dictum, it is hard to believe the bulk of his readers, unless they were widely different from the average humanity of all ages, really prized above the progress of the story. Mrs. Elizabeth Carter, who had strong views upon duelling, may have cared for the discussion upon that topic; and Miss Hester Mulso may have been interested in the pages dealing with parental authority; but we suspect that Mrs. Townly, the toast, and Mrs. Lutestring, the seamstress, were much more concerned to learn how Clarissa Harlowe would escape from Lovelace, and whether Clementina or Harriet Byron would ultimately succeed in marrying Sir Charles. And if these things were felt by the author's first unjaded readers, they must be felt more than ever by the readers of to-day, who, having come into a not inconsiderable inheritance of fiction in the interim,[1] are by no means bound to burden themselves with the defects and superfluities of the pioneers in the art. It may be, as it is sometimes asserted, that there is a growing reaction in favour of 'the Richardsonian

---

[1] At present about 1500 novels per annum (*Times Supplement*, 25th July 1902).

method, and that the readers of our time, wearied with snippets and summaries, are about to turn once more to the copious and pedestrian pages of the Father of the English Novel. We doubt it. That there is an extraordinary quality about that nerveless, ambling, redundant style of his which, to those who persevere, gradually absorbs and fascinates, may readily be granted. Nevertheless, the conditions of modern life would appear to be hopelessly averse from the perusal of novels in seven or eight volumes, which novels, moreover, in spite of their admitted *longueurs et langueurs*, appear to defy compression.

But if, as we think, Richardson's popularity with the public of the circulating library is never likely to revive again, his popularity is certain with the few — with those who, like Horace Walpole, either read what nobody else does, or, like Edward FitzGerald and Dr. Jowett, read only what takes their fancy. He must always find readers, too, with the students of literature. He was the pioneer of a new movement; the first certificated practitioner of sentiment; the English Columbus of the analytical novel of ordinary life. Before him, no one had essayed in this field to describe the birth and growth of a new impression, to show the ebb and flow of emotion in a mind distraught, to follow the progress of a passion, to dive so deeply into the human heart as to leave — in Scott's expressive words — " neither head, bay, nor inlet behind him until he had traced its soundings, and laid it down in his chart, with all its minute sinuosities, its depths and shallows." Added to this, there was a something in his nervous, high-strung constitution — a feminine streak as it were — which made him an unrivalled

anatomist of female character. He seems to have
known women more intimately and instinctively than
any deceased author we can recall, and he has written
of them with an interest, a patience, a discrimination,
and a sustained power of microscopic inquiry which
no author has surpassed. And they deserved it, for
he was also deeply indebted to them. " Knowing
something of the female heart," he tells Pastor Stinstra,
" I could not be an utter stranger to that of man."
The phrase betrays more than he intended. He knew
women; and through women he got his knowledge of
men with its concomitant defects. What Hazlitt calls
his " strong matter-of-fact imagination " did all the rest.

With the unprecedented vogue of Richardson during
the literary years of his life, it might be supposed that
he would be succeeded by a host of imitators. In his
own country, however, his influence is not so markedly
perceptible as it might have been, had his genius been
less individual, and his artistic method more worthy of
emulation. With him, no doubt, the stream of sentiment has its original fount and origin; but its course
was modified by other tendencies, and diverted into
different channels. Hence, it is not entirely easy to
point to this or that writer, and especially to this or
that great writer who follows, and to say that he was
largely energised by the author of *Sir Charles Grandison*
and *Clarissa*. Sterne no doubt came after him, and
Sterne, too, dealt, among other things, with sentiment.
But, at its best, Sterne's sentiment is sentiment with a
difference — a sentiment of an essence far subtler than
anything in Richardson, and smiling, with a queer con-
tortion, through its tears. Of Brooke's *Fool of Quality*
— that inconceivably tiresome book which Kingsley

praises for its "grand ethics," and its "absence of sentimentalism" [?] — it may indeed be affirmed that it shows the influence of Richardson, since it abounds both in weeping and moralities;[1] and something of the same kind may be advanced of Henry Mackenzie's *Man of Feeling*, except that if Mackenzie is the disciple of Richardson, he has absorbed him through Sterne.[2] Both the *Man of Feeling* and the *Fool of Quality* have, however, as pointed out by Miss Thomson, one affinity with Richardson, — they are preoccupied with questions of education, although this, as she is also careful to note, they may owe to Rousseau. But neither Mackenzie (in the *Man of Feeling*), nor Brooke, chose the epistolary style for their performances, as did that avowed Richardsonian, Miss Burney. Richardson's novels had been the passion of her (Miss Burney's) girlhood, and her first book, *Evelina*, is written in letters. But although Johnson protested that there were passages in it which might do honour to the author of *Clarissa*, he also, by comparing her Holborn beau to Fielding, indicated sufficiently that Richardson's influence was intermixed with other influences which

[1] Brooke is occasionally almost reminiscent of Richardson. Of his hero, Harry Clinton, a character says: — "Let me go, let me go from this place. The boy will absolutely kill me if I stay any longer. He overpowers, he suffocates me with the weight of his sentiments." This is quite in the Harriet Byron vein: — "O my Aunt! be so good as to let the servants prepare my apartments at Selby House. There is no living within the blazing glory of this man."

[2] The introduction nevertheless seems intended to suggest kinship with Richardson: — "Had the name of a Marmontel or a *Richardson* been on the title-page, 'tis odds that I should have wept." Mackenzie's *Julia de Roubigné*, it may be added, is in letters.

saved her from succumbing entirely to sensibility. In
Miss Burney's successor, Miss Austen, we are again
confronted with that writer's admiration for the author
of her youth. She had him by heart, we are told.
" Her knowledge of Richardson's works " — wrote her
nephew and biographer, the Rev. S. E. Austen-Leigh,
in 1870 — " was such as no one is likely again to
acquire, now that the multitude and the merits of our
light literature have called off the attention of readers
from that great master." But, although Miss Austen
too chose the " epistolary style" for the first form
of *Sense and Sensibility*, the connection between her
delicate craftsmanship and that of Richardson is
not very manifest. Whatever she got from him
must have been sublimed into something rarer and
more refined, leaving nothing appreciable except the
common attributes of minute imagination and mental
analysis.

One of the causes which no doubt tended to diminish
or modify the influence of Richardson in his own
country, was the fact that Fielding and Smollett were
also exerting considerable influence in a different
direction. But in France, where Fielding (in spite
of Mr. Defreval) was imperfectly understood, and
Smollett almost unknown, and where Marivaux had
already prepared the ground for the novel of
analysis, Richardson's welcome was immediate and
unmistakable. Aided, in some measure, by that gentle
Gallicising to which his " parts of speech " had been
subjected, he at once obtained a currency which was
absolutely unexampled, especially when it is remembered that France and England were, for the moment,
politically opposed, and that Richardson's preface to

Pamela, in the words of the *Journal de Police*,[1] was
"an insult to the entire French nation." In July
1742 Crébillon told Lord Chesterfield that, without
Pamela, the Parisians would not know what to read
or to say. How the book was dramatised and
imitated, has already been told in Chapter ii. *Clarissa*
was even more successful ; and by the time *Grandison*
appeared, in the words of the late M. Joseph Texte (to
whose admirable chapter on Richardson's influence in
France we at this point cheerfully acknowledge our
obligations), " admiration had become infatuation."
The colossal *Éloge* of Diderot in Suard's *Journal
Étranger* (1761) indicates the culminating point. In
seventeen pages of breathless eulogy,[2] thrown off at a
burst, Diderot dilates upon his theme. With much of
this magniloquent rhapsody it is now difficult to sym-
pathise, though of its sincerity there can be no doubt.
Diderot was wrong — as M. Texte points out — in
vaunting the purity of *Clarissa* at the expense of
certain French writers ; in preferring its author before
Montaigne, Nicole, and La Rochefoucauld for his
knowledge of the human heart, and in commending
him for a delicacy of art in which he is obviously
deficient. But at least he had read him, he admired
him enthusiastically, and he seized his distinctive

---

[1] The reference is apparently to the passage from Mr.
Defreval's letter, thus impartially rendered by Prévost : — "Tu
[*Pamela*] pourras servir de modèle aux écrivains d'une nation
voisine, qui auront l'occasion maintenant de recevoir en bon
argent sterling, à la place de la fausse monnaie qui a eu si
long-tems cours parmi nous dans des pièces ou l'on ne trouve
que la légèreté de cette inconstante nation." (*Œuvres de
Prévost*, Paris, 1784, i. xvi.). Why Prévost did not modify or
soften this injudicious passage, is difficult to understand.

[2] Assézat's edition, 1875, vol. v.

characteristics. His admiration will not even admit
that he is wearisome. " You accuse him of being
tedious ! Have you then forgotten the trouble, the
attention, the manœuvring that are necessary before the humblest enterprise can be brought to a
successful issue — before a lawsuit can be ended, a
marriage arranged, a reconciliation effected ? Think
what you please of these details; but they will be
interesting to me, if they are true, if they call the
passions into play, if they exhibit character. 'They
are commonplace,' say you; 'this is what we see
every day ?' You are wrong; it is what happens
every day before your eyes, without your ever per-
ceiving it. . . . Know that it is upon this multitude
of little things that illusion depends : it is very difficult
to imagine them : it is harder still to reproduce them."
There is more : — of Richardson's analytic power, —
of his fascination for the writer. " O Richardson,
Richardson — man unique in my eyes, you shall be my
reading at all times ! " Forced by necessity, he will
sell his books. But Richardson he will keep — on the
same shelf as Moses, Homer, Euripides, and Sophocles ;
and he will study them by turns.

Diderot praised Richardson because Richardson confirmed his own theories; Voltaire, on the other hand,
and despite his own effort of *Nanine*, depreciated him
because his views were opposed to those which he
himself advocated. But, in 1760, just a year before
Richardson's death had prompted the dithyrambs of
Diderot, appeared a novel by a writer as great as either,
La Nouvelle Héloïse. That Rousseau was influenced by
Richardson, that he went beyond him in style, that he
imported into his pages a nature-worship which he had

certainly not found in his model, that he had built
upon Richardson's basis with greater genius — are
things which need not here be repeated. "Richardson"
— says M. Texte — "wrote a novel; and Rousseau
writes a poem. The one is a very great novelist, but a
very bad writer; the other is an incomparable artist
in words. The one has no style at all; the other has
renewed the French language from its foundation."

This is the modern view.[1] But as Richardson's
novels during his life-time had been preferred, even in
France, to the performances of Le Sage and Prévost
and Marivaux, so after his death their popularity
was but little affected by the masterpiece of Rousseau.
He continued to be, as he had been, the model of the
Anglo-maniacs, and the English novel remained the
fashion in France for many years to come. As late as
1785 a French critic was found to write — "Clarissa,
the greatest among English novels, has also become
the first among our own." And long after he ceased to
be imitated, he continued to have admirers in Rousseau's country, and admirers of the greatest, from
Chateaubriand and André Chénier to George Sand
and Alfred de Musset — Alfred de Musset, for whom
Clarissa was "*le premier Roman du Monde.*"

Of a very definite kind was also Richardson's influence in Germany. Gellert the fabulist, as already
mentioned, translated *Pamela* and *Sir Charles Grandison,* and came no whit behind Diderot in panegyric.

---

[1] It was not, of course, the view of the *Critical Review* for
September 1761, which compared the two writers. Nor was it
Richardson's, who is said to have decorated his own version
of the *New Eloisa* with anything but notes of admiration.
(Nichols's *Anecdotes,* 1812, iv. p. 598.)

Richardson's works, he wrote, were imperishable : — they were nature, taste, and religion.   Immortal as was Homer among Christians, Richardson was more immortal still.   Gellert went further; he emulated Richardson in a long novel called *Das Leben der Schwedischen Gräfin von G.*   Hermes, Wieland, and a host of minor imitators, of whom the histories may be found in Erich Schmidt,[1] followed suit, and, like the French, they too carried Richardson to the stage. Wieland took Clementina for the theme of a tragedy; and Lessing's epoch-making drama of *Miss Sara Sampson,* among other English influences, clearly betrays the study of *Clarissa,* while Coleridge traces Richardson in the *Robbers* of Schiller.   Lastly, in the *Grandison der Zweite* of Musæus, he suffered the penalty of Teutonic parody.

[1] *Richardson, Rousseau und Göthe,* 1875.

INDEX

P

ENGLISH MEN OF LETTERS

EDITED BY

JOHN MORLEY

Cloth. 12mo. Price, 40 cents, each

ADDISON. By W. J. Courthope.

BACON. By R. W. Church.

BENTLEY. By Prof. Jebb.

BUNYAN. By J. A. Froude.

BURKE. By John Morley.

BURNS. By Principal Shairp.

BYRON. By Prof. Nichol.

CARLYLE. By Prof. Nichol.

CHAUCER. By Prof. A. W. Ward.

COLERIDGE. By H. D. Traill.

COWPER. By Goldwin Smith.

DEFOE. By W. Minto.

DE QUINCEY. By Prof. Masson.

DICKENS. By A. W. Ward.

DRYDEN. By G. Saintsbury.

FIELDING. By Austin Dobson.

GIBBON. By J. Cotter Morison.

GOLDSMITH. By William Black.

GRAY. By Edmund Gosse.

HUME. By T. H. Huxley.

JOHNSON. By Leslie Stephen.

KEATS. By Sidney Colvin.

LAMB. By Alfred Ainger.

LANDOR. By Sidney Colvin.

LOCKE. By Prof. Fowler.

MACAULAY.
By J. Cotter Morison.

MILTON. By Mark Pattison.

POPE. By Leslie Stephen.

SCOTT. By R. H. Hutton.

SHELLEY. By J. A. Symonds.

SHERIDAN. By Mrs. Oliphant.

SIR PHILIP SIDNEY.
By J. A. Symonds.

SOUTHEY. By Prof. Dowden.

SPENSER. By R. W. Church.

STERNE. By H. D. Traill.

SWIFT. By Leslie Stephen.

THACKERAY. By A. Trollope.

WORDSWORTH.
By F. W. H. Myers.

NEW VOLUMES

Cloth. 12mo. Price, 75 cents net

GEORGE ELIOT. By Leslie Stephen.

WILLIAM HAZLITT. By Augustine Birrell.

MATTHEW ARNOLD. By Herbert W. Paul.

JOHN RUSKIN. By Frederic Harrison.

ALFRED TENNYSON. By Alfred Lyall.

ENGLISH MEN OF LETTERS

EDITED BY

JOHN MORLEY

THREE BIOGRAPHIES IN EACH VOLUME

Cloth. 12mo. Price, $1.00, each

CHAUCER. By Adolphus William Ward. **SPENSER.** By R. W. Church. **DRYDEN.** By George Saintsbury.

MILTON. By Mark Pattison, B.D. **GOLDSMITH.** By William Black. **COWPER.** By Goldwin Smith.

BYRON. By John Nichol. **SHELLEY.** By John Addington Symonds. **KEATS.** By Sidney Colvin, M.A.

WORDSWORTH. By F. W. H. Myers. **SOUTHEY.** By Edward Dowden. **LANDOR.** By Sidney Colvin, M.A.

LAMB. By Alfred Ainger. **ADDISON.** By W. J. Courthope. **SWIFT.** By Leslie Stephen.

SCOTT. By Richard H. Hutton. **BURNS.** By Principal Shairp. **COLERIDGE.** By H. D. Traill.

HUME. By T. H. Huxley, F.R.S. **LOCKE.** By Thomas Fowler. **BURKE.** By John Morley.

FIELDING. By Austin Dobson. **THACKERAY.** By Anthony Trollope. **DICKENS.** By Adolphus William Ward.

GIBBON. By J. Cotter Morison. **CARLYLE.** By John Nichol. **MACAULAY.** By J. Cotter Morison.

SIDNEY. By J. A. Symonds. **DE QUINCEY.** By David Masson. **SHERIDAN.** By Mrs. Oliphant.

POPE. By Leslie Stephen. **JOHNSON.** By Leslie Stephen. **GRAY.** By Edmund Gosse.

BACON. By R. W. Church. **BUNYAN.** By J. A. Froude. **BENTLEY.** By R. C. Jebb.

PUBLISHED BY

THE MACMILLAN COMPANY

66 FIFTH AVENUE, NEW YORK